F

6/08

3.0

MEMORIES
of NINETY YEARS

MEMORIES

of NINETY YEARS

·PRINCESS ALICE, DUCHESS *of* GLOUCESTER·

C&B

COLLINS & BROWN

ACKNOWLEDGEMENT

In compiling this book I have drawn on my previous volume of Memoirs. I would like to thank my family for allowing me to reproduce illustrations from their photographic albums. I am also most grateful to John Sebastian McEwen for his help in editing the manuscript.

First published in Great Britain in 1991
by Collins & Brown Limited
Mercury House
195 Knightsbridge
London SW7 1RE

A CIP catalogue record for this book
is available from the British Library

Hardback ISBN 1 85585 048 6
Paperback ISBN 1 85585 039 7
Conceived, edited and designed by Collins & Brown Limited

Picture Research: Julia Browne
Designed by: David Fordham
Filmset by Bookworm Typesetting, Manchester
Reproduction by La Cromolito, Milan, Italy
Printed and bound in Italy by New Interlitho SpA

CONTENTS

Boughton.

Alice. 1904.

PART ONE

Childhood

A family group taken at Montagu House on 9 July 1894, seven years before I was born. The occasion was the eighty-second birthday of my great-grandmother, Louisa, Duchess of Abercorn.

8

Chapter One

MONTAGU HOUSE

 ornament

SOME YEARS AGO IN MY ROLE AS AIR chief commandant of the WRAF I found myself addressing a gathering of air women in the Ministry of Defence and startled them by revealing that I had been born just below where we were all sitting — in my mother's corner bedroom overlooking the Thames, a room that I can remember well. She must have found the timing of my arrival very inconvenient — Christmas Day, 1901.

Can it really be ninety years ago? The ladies of the WRAF were right to look astonished for, of course, I did not make my first appearance in this world in a government office but in another house entirely — in Montagu House, the large Whitehall building that had been the London home of my family for centuries. Nothing remains of it today, not even the name. All I can say is that it was one of several, large, private houses then in Whitehall and stood more or less opposite the entrance to Horse Guards Parade, where tourists today gather round the mounted guardsmen who stand sentry at the gate. The sentry duty at least has not changed, but the house we spied from was pulled down more than sixty years ago to make way for government offices.

Myself aged two on Vixen.

One of the Dukes of Montagu originally built the house to save him the journey to his principal residence in Bloomsbury when he was kept late at the House of Lords. We hear so much about muggings and other horrors in London today but at least we can take some comfort in knowing that we live in more peaceful times. To travel a mile through the streets after dark in the seventeenth century was clearly considered so dangerous as to be out of the question. Our ancestors, even the most privileged of them, lived much rougher lives than we do. My great grandfather was enrolled as a Special Constable during the Chartist riots in 1848 and received a nasty wound in his side during an affray at the end of Westminster Bridge. It was a serious injury, the wound remaining open for many months. Apparently he also had an enormous lump on his head from being butted by his horse out hunting. It used to make his head ache when he went shooting.

I am indebted for these tales to a book of family memoirs entitled *The Fleeting Opportunity* by my uncle Lord George Scott. He also provides the following interesting information about my great grandfather's business affairs, particularly with regard to Montagu House.

RIGHT: *The garden at Montagu House. In the background is the wall over which we dangled spiders and through the trees you can see the river Thames.*

He seldom made mistakes, but two large investments were financial failures, namely the building of Granton harbour, for which he mortgaged his estates up to over £700,000, and the building of Montagu House.

The Crown lease of old Montagu House expired, and the conditions for a fresh ninety-nine years' lease were that he should spend £80,000. He actually spent £120,000. Chesterfield House with its huge garden (including the whole of the present-day Chesterfield Gardens) was for sale freehold. Burn, the architect, advised him to buy it, and made plans to suit his requirements if he should wish to enlarge the house. This freehold estate could have been bought and the additions completed for the sum he spent on a ninety-nine years' lease of Montagu House. I was told that he was over-persuaded by busybodies, against his better judgment.

Montagu House was a large building overlooking the Thames, with a big garden extending to the Embankment and a gravel sweep at the front, with trees hiding the house from the traffic as it passed along Whitehall. There was a porter's lodge and railings and a grand entrance gate. The two top floors were devoted to bedrooms, the first floor to sitting-rooms and reception rooms and the ground floor to the kitchens and servants' quarters. The main reception rooms all gave on to a wide stone terrace, with steps at either end descending to the garden. There were no attics or basement.

My own memories of Montagu House, which cover the first decade of our century and thus follow on from those of my uncle, are of a very large house, which of course it was. There must have been a great number of bedrooms for during the summer season not only my parents and, eventually, the eight of us children stayed there, but also my Aunt Katie Hampden (my father's eldest sister) and her husband and children. There were also, of course, my grandparents and my Aunt Connie, their second youngest child, who, before her marriage to Douglas Cairns, acted as a general factota to her parents. The grown-ups each had a maid or valet. Two nurses, a nursery-maid and a governess supervised me and my brothers and sisters. All told there were sixty-eight people permanently resident during the season — and, as far as I know, only one bathroom in the whole building. I cannot remember who was allowed to use it!

Duchess Dow. of Abercorn's descendants in Garden
Montagu House. July 8th 1894

11

Myself and my cousin David Brand. During the summer months the Brand cousins occupied the other nursery at Montagu House.

Alice. David. 1908

Our nurseries and schoolroom were on the second floor, alongside the other main bedrooms and dressing-rooms. Aunt Katie's children, the Brand cousins, had their nurseries on the top floor with a wonderful view over the Embankment and the river. One could hear the trams rattling past and the booming and hoots of the ships travelling up and down the Thames.

My grandparents I can remember in some ways better than I can my parents. This is not altogether surprising. My father was an MP and rarely got home before our bedtime, and my mother hated the season. She was a shy, retiring person, who never came to the nurseries and always seemed to be busy in her own little sitting-room or lying on a sofa with a headache. Occasionally we would be allowed in, but one always had to be quiet and do a jigsaw puzzle or something equally boring. On the whole, as young children, we seldom saw our parents; indeed the nursery seldom even saw the schoolroom, to which we went when we were aged about eight. They were worlds apart.

My grandmother, in contrast, could not possibly have been more sociable. She entertained enormously, with masses of friends and relations pouring in and out for lunch parties and dinner parties. There was the custom, apparently established by my great-grandparents, that anyone who knew the family could turn up for lunch without invitation. My Aunt Connie, in a private memoir she wrote, says that this custom was very popular with the denizens of Whitehall, from prime ministers downwards, and that up to twenty extra guests were catered for daily. I recall only two extra places being laid in this way —

perhaps entertainment was already becoming less lavish. It was a nice custom, especially for people who were not well off. There were always huge lunch parties and the two empty chairs were invariably filled.

Once we had left the nursery and entered the schoolroom, and were therefore considered to know how to behave, we were allowed to have lunch in the dining-room. The schoolroom table was set apart from the table for the grown-ups, tucked away in a distant corner. There we sat with a governess and had to wait our turn till the grown-ups had been helped, which took ages. If there were treats, like strawberries and cream, we would suffer agonies in case they were finished before reaching us. The butlers and footmen always tried to make sure there was something left over for us.

At one such pre-war lunch I remember that for the first time in my life I saw a woman — the morganatic wife of the Grand Duke Michael of Russia — smoke a cigarette. She fitted the cigarette into the end of a long holder and then, to our amazement, had it lit. Nor was that all. My mother, who was presiding, had ordered mince, which she was keen on for some reason. When the dish was offered to the Grand Duke he said, very haughtily, 'No thank you. I prefer to chew my own meat.'

One memorable evening we were woken up at about 10 p.m. to watch my grandparents going off to some court function in the Buccleuch state coach. My grandmother was Mistress of the Robes to Queen Alexandra. The coach was ornate and magnificent and was only used for important occasions like court balls or the Opening of Parliament. The harness was shining silver and there were a wigged coachman and footman in front and two postilions behind — all in livery, with red breeches and white stockings. The family coat-of-arms, picked out in fairy-lights, had been mounted for the occasion over the front door. I remember distinctly this being lit electrically, though I do not think there was electric lighting in the house at that date. The coach subsequently went to a museum in Maidstone, but today it can be seen at Boughton in Northamptonshire, another Buccleuch residence in England. (My nephew Johnnie, the present Duke, has been trying to find some stuffed horses for it so that the public can see the magnificent uniforms and harness as they were intended to be seen, but so far he has met with no success.)

Each morning at Montagu House we used to visit our grandparents. My grandmother would be in her lovely sitting-room, with its blue satin covered chairs. She always looked very sedate. My grandfather usually gave us half a crown or a sweet. We just went in and said 'Good Morning' before our morning walk; then we would scamper down the huge, slippery, white marble staircase into the hall. The hall was paved with white marble inlaid with black corners, and we used to enjoy jumping from one of these black 'islands' to the next. Footmen, wearing livery, sat on two mahogany benches, ready to open the door or answer bells. The prams were hidden somewhere to one side and the footmen used to help our nurses down the steps with them. A troop of little Scotts would then cross Whitehall and go into St James's Park to feed the ducks, making faces on the way at the mounted sentries who were always on guard at the entrance to Horse Guards Parade.

There were eight of us in our family and being so many we tended to pair off by age. In order of birth there were Margaret or 'Mida', Walter, Billy, Sybil, me, Mary, Angela and George. Mida was born in 1892 and Angela in 1906, so one of us must have appeared almost every other year — except for George, who was born in 1911 and was therefore very much younger than the rest of us. I really hardly knew my eldest brother and sister. Sybil was my main companion and guardian angel except, that is, when Billy came home from the holidays and she abandoned me for this older and more exciting company. Mary was the wildest in the family and much the prettiest and most attractive of us as a child.

I and my four sisters were invariably dressed alike in spite of the fourteen years' difference between the eldest and the youngest, and clothes were very much handed down. Mary outgrew me in time so I became fourth on the clothes list instead of third. You just had to put up with what you inherited. As far as I know all our clothes came from Gorringe's, a children's clothes shop in Sloane Street; but no doubt there were other sources of supply. We certainly had no say in the matter. When I look at old photographs and see those ridiculous hats we had to wear and the sheer volume of the many layered little dresses, I cannot imagine how we put up with it. I do not remember being stifling hot, but we often must have been. I certainly do not remember ever being allowed to take anything off.

On wet days, for our trips to the park, we were put into little red mackintoshes, which caused great amusement as we marched past the soldiers because when it was raining they wore the same. Our prams, like the various household carriages, were adorned with the family crest and painted in the Buccleuch colours: dark green with a pale green line. The Fitzwilliam family, who lived next door in Richmond Terrace (alas, no more), had yellow prams and carriages, which we thought much smarter and envied greatly.

Mr Shotter was our lodge-keeper, an impeccably dressed old gentleman in a top hat. He would open the main gates in answer to a push-bell, but a side-gate for people entering on foot could be opened automatically by treading on a little pedal outside. It was always a great game to tread on this pedal and hide out of sight before Mr Shotter could spot us — although the arrival of a breathless nanny or governess in hot pursuit gave a clue to the culprits. Mr Shotter was a true friend, who always played his part as a man baffled by an inexplicable mystery with gusto.

Occasionally we would be taken for a drive with our mother to drop visiting cards. It was the custom to thank one's host and hostess the day after a party by dropping cards. Usually the coachman and footman would be dispatched to do this, but occasionally, probably because she had nothing better to do, my mother, taking some of us with her, went along also. There was a very precise etiquette involved. One large card and two little ones had to be left, twisted over. The large one had 'The Countess of Dalkeith' engraved on it, the smaller ones 'The Earl of Dalkeith' — two 'Earls' had to go with one 'Countess' for some reason. No message was written on the cards. The

My father and mother. As young children we seldom
saw our parents.

footman would jump off and, on entering the particular house, would leave the cards on a tray provided in the hall. Meanwhile we would sit waiting in the carriage.

Other times, after tea, my mother would take us to Hyde Park in the landau, an open carriage with a hood that could go up if it rained. We would stop near Hyde Park Corner and go and sit on little green metal chairs that were set out under the trees. One hired the use of these uncomfortable seats by buying a ticket for tuppence from a ticket collector. Each day had a different colour, so that people could not cheat by using the same ticket twice. Various boring old gentlemen in top hats and tailcoats would then perch themselves alongside my mother and make polite conversation. We viewed the whole procedure with a certain amount of dread. One evening as we plop-plopped along in the shadow of the fat coachman and the thin footman, this ritual was transformed by the sudden appearance of a fire-engine, with bells ringing, pulled by six black horses at full gallop. Our fat horses, spurred on by the unexpected competition, tried their best to follow and were only checked with difficulty. It was a rather alarming moment.

Our greatest enjoyment was the garden. We were allowed in there at any time whereas it seemed the grown-ups never went if they could help it. On one side of the lawn was a beautiful Chinese pagoda, now at Boughton, in which my grandparents used to take tea, weather permitting; otherwise we seemed to have the whole place to ourselves. There were a few large plane trees, a catalpa tree, bushes and bordering flower-beds. The flowers were for the most part red geraniums and marguerites encircled by close-planted clumps of those little royal-blue plants one always sees in public gardens. All other London gardens that we visited looked exactly the same. At the far end there was a thick line of shrubs, a narrow path and then, bordering the Embankment, a seven-foot wall with a wide top. We children — thought to be safely out of mischief in the garden — would pile chairs against it and clamber up to watch the passing traffic on the street and the ships beyond, which were much more numerous in those days. We dangled wobbly wire spiders on long bits of elastic in the path of pedestrians below, skilfully whisking them up and ducking out of sight before our victims could spot us. There were always a number of pavement-artists sitting opposite, who could not have provided a more appreciative

Mary. Alice.
Sybil. Walter. Lala. Billy. 1909

The Scott children in 1909 with only George yet to be born.

audience for our escapades. Afterwards we carefully put back the chairs exactly where we had found them. The garden had other attractions. Near the wall we each had a little allotment to tend. To get into the garden we had to go along a narrow passage past the housekeeper's room. This was always a treat because she would let us choose something from the store of her chocolates as we passed.

On Sundays we were taken to church in the private chapel at Marlborough House. Queen Alexandra was usually there. She gave a children's party every year and at one of them a lot of pygmies danced about naked, which we thought very funny. For weeks afterwards my sister Sybil and I used to get into trouble for jumping about without any clothes on when we should have been tucked up for the night. On the whole we did not do much visiting or party going. Our numbers made us self-sufficient and never at a loss for amusement.

A memorable pastime was to send semaphore flag signals from the schoolroom balcony to the policemen across the way in Scotland Yard.

They jovially signalled answers to our messages. Government offices were already predominant in the district when Montagu House was taken over as an adjunct to the War Office in the second year of the Great War. There are some photographs in Mida's book of some event in the summer of 1915, which I recognise as having taken place in the garden. King George and Queen Mary are there and at first I thought it was Buckingham Palace, but the curved steps from the terrace show it to be Montagu House (those at the Palace are straight). But what we were doing I cannot imagine. There are posters proclaiming 'Vive la France' so I presume it must have been some fund-raising event to do with the war. It may well have been the last function to take place at the house and, as far as we know, is one of only two photographs now in existence that record what it looked like, even so unhelpfully. After that final summer my parents made do with a flat, before buying 2 Grosvenor Place towards the end of the war. By then the world too had changed out of all recognition.

Walter. Mida. 1903.

Sybil. Mamma. Mida. Walter. Billy. FILEY. 1903.

*As young children our seaside holidays were often
spent at Filey on the Yorkshire coast. Aged two I
must have been tucked up in my pram.*

Chapter Two

EILDON HALL

WHEN THE LONDON SEASON CAME to an end in July, Montagu House would be abandoned for another year and our family would disperse. My grandparents would go north to Drumlanrig in Dumfriesshire for the grouse shooting and my parents would take us back to our home — traditionally the home of the Buccleuch son and heir — at Eildon Hall, at the foot of the three Eildon Hills, in the Scottish Borders.

This journey north was always a source of the keenest excitement, though rather long and tedious for a child. A happy moment came when the train used to stop somewhere south of Penrith to fill up with water, and our nanny would open the window and let us hang our heads out to breathe in the first delicious scent of the moors, while the engine up ahead hissed gently in the silence. Amongst clumps of heather, the bog cotton and little wild flowers — scabious and hare bells (which we call bluebells north of the border) — bobbed in the breeze and we knew that our journey would soon be over and we would be safe home in Scotland. All of us were fervent nationalists: everything Scottish was wonderful, everything English quite dreadful.

Perhaps because Eildon was the first grown-up

Apart from the ponies, outdoor life at Eildon was centred on the foxhound puppies, who arrived each year to be 'walked'.

home of aspiring Dukes of Buccleuch, and has therefore always been a young family's house, it has a charmingly domestic air. The house was bought by my family in 1838 and is a very neat Georgian building in the local coral-pink sandstone. It stands 600 feet above sea level and commands a wondrous view of the valley below and the Merse beyond, which stretches away to the Cheviots 30 miles distant — the range of hills that for centuries has acted as the border between England and Scotland. Across these fields and woods the colour would be forever changing under the sun and the shadows of the clouds.

My Aunt Connie describes it in her memoirs as becoming more Edwardian in its decoration with the arrival of my parents — 'more photographs in silver frames', as she puts it — but there were no structural changes.

I remember as a three-year-old finding the stairs a long, exhausting climb, then later rushing up at a great rate. Now, at eight-nine, I find they have returned to their original height! Once I am in the nurseries all intervening years vanish. The same smell that I have always known, dominates. No matter how floors and walls are treated — from shabby carpet in my nursery days, followed by linoleum or cork carpet (both of which have a

A meet at Eildon. In the foreground is my father wearing a hat: in the background is one of the Eildon hills. I may be one of the two girls peering over the rhododendrons.

revolting smell), and now pretty and good carpets – the familiar smell joyfully greets my nostrils. What it is, I know not – possibly the wood of doors.

How familiar such sensations must be to all of us who return to the haunts of our childhood in later years.

My earliest memory of all is of Eildon. I am in the nursery having a bath in a tin tub. Two brothers rush in fighting and one kicks off a boot which lands with a splash in the water. The nursery-maid is furious. That must have been when I was two.

Eildon was very safe for children and we could run wherever we liked. This we were no doubt encouraged to do in the relative absence of our parents. My father was the local MP and equally occupied by his directorships of the North British Railway and the Bank of Scotland, so we

A sketch of Eildon through the trees that I painted in 1921.

seldom saw him except for lunch on Sunday. Our mother was at home but my memories of her are equally few. She sat on the sofa and sewed a lot. Looking back, I suppose quite often she must have been resting from having one baby or preparing to have another. Expectant mothers in those days were very often encouraged to be inactive. Lady Home, the mother of Alec Home, the Prime Minister, used to insist on being pushed about in a wheelchair for the full nine months. My mother did make a point of seeing us in the drawing-room for an hour after tea each day, for which we had to change into smarter frocks. On these occasions she would sometimes play the piano and sing or even whistle some tune to us, which we loved.

People seldom came to stay, except for Uncle Henry – Lord Henry Scott – my father's younger brother and our only bachelor uncle. Uncle

FILEY

1905

Tommy Brand. Alice.

Mamma. Billy. Tommy. Sybil.

Mary. Alice. Sybil.

Mamma. Tommy. Sybil.

 *A later holiday at Filey. Aged four I am pictured
with another of my numerous Brand cousins,
Tommy. What clothes we wore!*

19

Lunch at Eildon during the visit by King George V and Queen Mary to the Borders in 1923. My brother Walter and family then occupied the house.

Henry was a very keen horseman and was allowed to use Eildon as his headquarters during the hunting season. The house was well situated for this, being only three miles from the Buccleuch Hunt kennels. Two of Uncle Henry's cronies — William and Cospatrick Douglas-Home, Alec Douglas-Home's uncles — were also regular visitors because they took a nearby house for the season opposite the Buccleuch Arms in St Boswells. St Boswells was also where Uncle Henry stabled his hunters. Two days a week Uncle Henry and Cospatrick disappeared into Edinburgh to do something at a bank and thought themselves very hard worked. The rest of the time they spent hunting, shooting or fishing, depending on the time of year.

Cospatrick always dropped in for lunch after he had been to church on Sundays. My father was a tease who got great pleasure from arguments and had no difficulty in setting off Uncle Henry and Cospatrick. The talk was usually political and of no interest to my mother. She would sit in silence at the end of the table while the gentlemen argued between themselves. The last thing she would have done was join in the debate. I doubt if she so much as ticked off even the youngest of housemaids in the whole course of her life; she was too

gentle and just would not have known what to say. Occasionally some elderly female relation provided her with company for a few days, but on the whole I fear she had a lonely time.

Uncle Henry was a good friend to us children and played a part in encouraging us to ride. Sybil and I loved riding more than anything. My father was not interested and my mother thought it dangerous, so outside encouragement was important to us. Luckily the Scotts in general were a hunting family. Uncle George Scott was Master of the Buccleuch at that date, and my brothers were also keen and helped us quite a lot. Walter, in time, was also to become Master of the Buccleuch.

All this support no doubt ensured that we soon had our own ponies. It was the custom for little girls to ride astride by then, but my mother did not think it proper for us to be seen in breeches so insisted we wore divided skirts instead. These flapped about and could not have been more uncomfortable for the animals as well as ourselves. Although my mother chiefly disliked our riding because she considered it dangerous, we used to wear nothing on our heads other than floppy blue felt hats. At that time no one seemed to think it necessary for

Miss Maffey. Alice. Sybil. Mary. 1912

Miss Maffey (our governess), myself, Sybil and Mary in a quarry in the Eildon hills. Her head for heights was later tested when Mary tried to push her out of the schoolroom window.

heads to be protected. I frequently fell on mine but never seemed any the worse for it. Nevertheless, we must have been a great worry for the groom, as we always went as fast as we could and only stopped when the ponies themselves thought it was best to do so.

Apart from the ponies and Jack Graham, our favourite groom who, alas, did not return from the First World War, outdoor life was centred on the foxhound puppies, who arrived each year to be 'walked'. They lived in the stables and had a tendency to escape into the garden. I think, looking back, that I was somewhat starved in my affections. These were transferred from my teddy bear to the puppies. Up until then I had prayed fervently every night for my teddy to come to life.

We used to enjoy the gardens at Eildon. Not only were there nice things to eat — lovely raspberries, peaches and figs — but the gardeners, with whom we were great friends, encouraged us to do our own gardening by giving us plants. These we would cosset in our own little plots. One holiday Billy made a wonderful rock garden in the wood. The work absorbed us for hours on end. Its chief glory was a splendid pool, which grew more and more impressive as the days went by. It was, therefore, a particularly calamitous moment when an angry farmer correctly identified this masterpiece as the reason for a growing and previously unexplained water shortage. Billy had diverted the local supply from his cows. No doubt we found solace in walking down to

the railway bridge and watching the trains, another Eildon treat. There was also a trout pond at the foot of the field in front of the house, which is now used by local anglers.

From the age of six, in term time, we would be in the schoolroom and spend most of the day with the governess. I cannot remember what we were taught. Very little, I should think. Reading, writing and simple sums. I think we did history, but not Scottish history. When we were bigger, German, French and sewing were added, and later still Italian; but with little permanent result. Today I can speak none of these languages. We used to go through governesses at a tremendous rate, which is hardly surprising when one recalls that my younger sister Mary — a beautiful, very strong child but with an all too easily aroused temper — once tried to push Miss Maffey an immensely tall governess, out of the window. The exception was 'Meggie'. She was a wonderful teacher and a sweet person, from whom I learned much that was a great help in later years.

Meggie was also very religious, her father and brothers all being clergymen, and insisted on morning prayers round the schoolroom table. When we were ready and kneeling she would ring a bell, at which signal the schoolroom footman would appear and have to join in. I am sure she did it purely for what she considered to be his own best interests, but as far as I was concerned it was always rather embarrassing.

Eva Trefusis.   Aunt Katie.   Grandmamma.   Lady Elphinstone.
DRUMLANRIG. 1911.

Afternoon at Drumlanrig. A favourite walk
was to the kitchen garden where there were
eight hundred yards of greenhouses to be
strolled through.

Chapter Three

DRUMLANRIG CASTLE

IN SEPTEMBER WE WOULD OFTEN BREAK our time at Eildon with a visit to my grandparents at Drumlanrig. There, in the autumn, my grandfather liked to organise shooting parties for his sons and relatives. Of all our homes Drumlanrig was for me the most beautiful — and that includes the countryside surrounding it. I am, of course, not alone in this. For many lovers of architecture it is the most beautiful house in Scotland and some have gone as far as the old Duke of Portland who wrote that 'it is the most glorious residence in the British Isles.' 'Glorious' is a good word for it. Set in its beautiful park with wooded hills all around and the wild moors beyond, it looks from the distance like a fairy castle — and never more so than in recent times when it can be floodlit at night. The river Nith winds through the park and you descend from the house through terraced gardens, the borders cut in fantastic shapes and separated from gravel paths by clipped box-hedges.

Drumlanrig did not origially belong to the Scott family. Immemorially it was the property of the Red Douglases and the present castle was built for a Douglas, the first Duke of Queensberry, at the end of the seventeenth century. Scotland, at that date, was just emerging from

Sybil. 1909.

My grandfather loved to have children around. Sybil and I were the lucky ones chosen to stay at Drumlanrig.

one of the most bloodthirsty periods of civil war in its history, and, as a result, Drumlanrig is an extraordinary cross between the palace of a sophisticated grandee and the defensive castle of a warrior chief. There are lovely sunny rooms looking out over the park; and then, at its four corners, towers containing dark and forbidding stone staircases up which one climbed to one's bedroom. On calm evenings one was lulled to sleep by the happy trotting of the Marr burn; but on stormy nights one lay in fear as the winds howled round the turrets. Outside the walls are built of pink granite and, when the sun shines after rain, the flecks of mica in the stone make the whole castle glitter like a jewel. The present castle is the work of the Scottish architect Sir William Bruce and came into the Buccleuch family through the marriage of Francis, the second Duke, to Lady Jane Douglas, daughter of the second Duke of Queensberry. On the death without issue of the last Duke of Queensberry in 1810, the title and property passed to the third Duke of Buccleuch, grandson of Lady Jane.

My grandfather loved to have children around and Sybil and I were more often than not the lucky ones chosen to be with him during his stays at Drumlanrig. The first time I was allowed to go

A view of Drumlanrig
from afar.

there must have been when I was about eight. We stayed, accompanied by a governess and maid, from October until the annual move to Dalkeith House for Christmas. The day formally began with prayers in the chapel. The Reverend Smith Dorrien officiated, a retired parson from the Church of England who used to act as a private chaplain when my grandparents were in residence. These prayers were attended by Aunt Connie, Mr Whitmore (my grandfather's secretary), the housekeeper, housemaids, us children and the governess. My grandparents and their guests only attended the Sunday service.

After lessons Sybil and I would joyfully set off on the morning ride. There were miles and miles of beautifully kept grass rides through the woods and along the bank of the Nith. It must have taken many estate workmen to cut the sward and remove the seedling trees. We could let our ponies go as fast as they wanted and when a ride divided, Sybil would go one way and I the other to the dismay of the groom who was there to look after us. Should he follow the elder girl on the spirited highbred pony or the younger one on the slower, more sedate animal? Luckily for him the rides usually coincided before we reached home. We loved galloping through those silent woods and past the small

lochs. Wild duck would spring up quacking loudly and often a roe deer or a red squirrel, which were numerous in those days, would cross our path. At one point there was a large group of monkey-puzzle trees, and we always hoped that one day we might see a monkey in their branches. Afternoons were left at our disposal and we would invent games and fight duels under the ancient yews below the castle or, if the burn was in spate we would watch the salmon and sea trout leaping the waterfall.

Most days the men would be out shooting — sometimes accompanied by us and a rather unwilling Reverend Smith Dorrien. They were usually after duck and pheasants but Uncle George describes a day when no less than ninety-three blackcocks were shot before lunch. Alas, today, this most handsome of gamebirds is a rare sight — not just in the west of Scotland but throughout the British Isles. My Scottish regiment, The King's Own Scottish Borderers (KOSB), traditionally have a blackcock's tail in their bonnets as the regimental insignia. They had hoped to refurbish all the bonnets with new tails for their tricentennial celebrations; but such is the shortage today that they were unable to do so and now have to resort to plastic replicas.

Uncle Henry. Papa. Grandmamma. Uncle George. Uncle
Aunt Connie. Mamma. Billy. Grand papa. Walter. Sybil.

LEFT: This family group was photographed at the annual cricket match at Langholm.

LEFT: This family group was photographed at the annual cricket match at Langholm.

BELOW LEFT: Myself in 1910 with my 'teddy bear' – the name had just been invented after Teddy Roosevelt, the US president.

While the shooting was in progress, drives around the countryside would be organised for the ladies of the party or any other non-combatants. Alternatively there were walks, including one to the kitchen garden, a mile away from the house, where there were 800 yards of greenhouses to be strolled through and a summer-house in which tea was sometimes held. If tea was in the castle, the ladies would have changed out of their heavy woollen day clothes into lighter tea gowns.

After tea the guests would rush about with us in games of hide and seek and pounce piggy — a Scott variation in which two people hid and ambushed the rest. They seemed to enjoy this as much as we did and I expect some were quite glad of an opportunity to take refuge in a dark cupboard or behind a thick curtain and enjoy a few secluded moments to themselves! The four

Alice.   1910

towers and three floors of long passages provided plenty of exercise, and we must have run miles during the course of an evening.

As for our grandparents, they usually played each other at billiards after tea and, if they saw that we had nothing more exciting to do, would often allow us to score for them. The task was not particularly exciting, but it had its compensation. When we scored patiently and correctly, my grandfather would tip us a golden half-sovereign: something most acceptable, since we were not given pocket-money of any kind.

At 7.15, after their rampage with us, guests would have been summoned to their rooms by the gong to bathe in the portable tubs prepared for them and to change for dinner. Every lady brought a maid, every gentleman a valet. The gong for dinner would be sounded at 8.15.

Another sound that comes back to me is the

gentle noise of the gravel being raked first thing in the mornings. This was done every day, whether the ground had been disturbed or not. Looking down from the nursery windows one would see rows of old men raking away. The estate employed almost a hundred gardeners then. Many of them were of an age that nowadays would mean retirement and probable exile from the countryside altogether; but in those days they would all have had stone cottages on or near the estate and lived happy and contented working lives to the end.

One of my favourite books as a child was *Froggie's Little Brother*. It was about a slum boy and used to make me weep every time I read it; but my own experience of working people could not have been more different. Everybody we knew was well looked after and their children were healthy and went to excellent village schools. In fact one of the things I should most like to convey of those times is how very, very nice all the servants (it hardly seems right to use such a word nowadays) were, and what real family friends they became. Indeed some of them were part of the family as far as we were concerned, having been connected with us for generations. Too often today one is given the impression that all landowners in the old days were selfish boors, with little concern for the well-being of those they employed.

Nevertheless the servants, not least the domestic servants with whom we came into daily contact, formed a separate world with its own clearly defined system of rules and manners. 'Below stairs' there was a ranking system just as precise in its protocol as the one upstairs. There was the steward's room, which was ruled by the house steward or butler and nicknamed the pug's parlour by the junior servants not privileged to enter it, and the servants' hall, which was a general meeting place for everyone who worked in the house. The head of the household was the steward, who controlled everything and everybody: from the setting of the clocks to the travelling arrangements of the guests; from the dismissal of staff to the organisation and restocking of the cellars. Next to the steward in seniority was the housekeeper, who looked after the arrangements of the lady guests and controlled the female staff. Then came the groom-of-the-bedchambers, who looked after the particular welfare of the guests. It was, for instance, part of his responsibility to check that the writing-tables were neat and in order every morning — every pencil sharpened, every pen-holder cleaned, every ink-well brimming and sand-shaker full. He also had to make sure that the flowers were watered and fresh. Finally there was the under-butler, the junior member of the ruling triumvirate of the male staff, who was in charge of the silver and the footmen, of whom there were usually no less than three.

The housemaids rose between 5 and 6 a.m. to sweep all the fireplaces and rooms before 9, after which they had to be as invisible as possible as they went about their duties. Carpets would all have been brushed with a broom and — least popular of household chores — the grates polished. The groom-of-the-bedchambers would supervise the gardeners, if the flowers were being restocked, and the odd-job man would scurry to and fro with baskets of logs. Later there would be the valeting to attend to, bells to be answered and the dining-room to prepare for the gentlemen's breakfast. Ladies breakfasted in bed. At some point the steward would pass by to make sure everything was in order. Meanwhile from 6 a.m. the kitchen-maids and still-room maids were busy preparing the various breakfasts for the dining-room, school-room, nursery, individual guests, steward's room and servants' hall.

A considerable etiquette had to be observed in the preparation of breakfast. The still-room maid was required to cook all the boiled eggs, except those for the guests breakfasting in the dining-room, but no other kind. Fried, poached, baked (a great favourite swimming in cream) and scrambled eggs were done in the kitchen. Nor, once the egg was boiled, did the still-room maid play any further part in its life. It then became the responsibility of another maid, who took it to the kitchen where the trays were prepared, before bearing it aloft to the appointed bedroom. No wonder, when news reached the nursery on one occasion that the second nursery maid was engaged to the groom-of-the-bedchambers, the housekeeper was heard to ask, 'Where ever can they have met?'

Of course still-room maids and kitchen-maids had many other duties. Everything to do with tea emanated from the still-room and every day after lunch the kitchen-maids scrubbed the floors of the kitchen, the scullery and all the larders, spreading fresh sawdust where necessary. The heavier job of cleaning the long basement passage was undertaken once a week by the odd-job men using deck-scrubbers.

There was said to be a ghost at Drumlanrig. My mother saw it as a young girl on her first visit to the house. She and her sister, the two beautiful Miss Bridgemans, were sent there — presumably thanks to the scheming of their mother and the Duchess of Buccleuch — in the hope that one of them would catch my father's eye. On their way to bed, the

Our grandparents usually played billiards after tea. When we scored for them correctly my grandfather would tip us a gold half sovereign: something most acceptable, since we were not given pocket money of any kind.

candle flames no doubt faltering from time to time in the draught of the passage, they saw something furry moving towards them. They were terrified. The candle blew out, but luckily they found the door of their bedroom, rushed in and, after their excited report at the time, never much liked to talk about it again. Then years later, after my mother had indeed become the Countess of Dalkeith, she was found looking pea-green in the hall one day by Lady Mabel Howard, who was staying as a guest. 'What's the matter with you!' exclaimed Lady Mabel. 'It's the most extraordinary thing,' replied my poor mother shakily. 'I saw a huge monkey sitting on the chair there.' 'My dear, you have must have eaten too much at lunch.' But no, my mother repeated that it was just the result of seeing the monkey and, as on the first occasion, insisted that nothing further should be made of it.

Shortly afterwards, during the war, Drumlanrig was turned into a hospital. One day the matron asked our agent's wife, who was running things, if she could speak to her on a matter of urgency. 'I saw something awful in the night,' she said as soon as they were alone, 'and I'm afraid I just can't stay.' So she left, and nobody knew why, but after the war someone was looking through the books in the muniment room and they

came on an inventory for the house in 1700. The matron's room had once been called 'Yellow Monkey or Haunted Room'. My only unpleasant memory of Drumlanrig is of having diphtheria there — a frightening disease in those days, before there was any known prevention against it or cure. It was presumed I must have contracted it on the train journey. Anyway, while I was in bed a little girl in a long frock came to me and I was mystified because her feet were four inches off the ground. No doubt I was delirious, but it would not surprise me if she really was the ghost of some child who had lived in that room generations before – her hovering could be explained by the floor having sunk since that distant time.

Otherwise my most lasting memory of the castle in those pre-war days is of Sybil. Thinking me inside the lavatory she said, 'I can see you but you can't see me' at which point the door, to her horror, opened and who should have emerged but the Reverend Smith Dorrien!

Annual visits came to an end in 1913, and made way for the conversation of the castle into a hospital. It was not until 1927 that the family returned to find life there transformed by the introduction of electric light, central heating and every modern convenience.

Mr Trotter   Major Logan Hume.   Lady C. Blackburn.   Mount stuart Elphinstone.
more. Mr Guild.   Aunt Connie.   Betsy Fitzwilliam. Aunt Katie. Uncle Herbert.   Mr Sherrin.
Uncle Laddo.   David Scott. Walter Mida. Charlie Scott. Maud Wyndham

The fancy dress Christmas dinner at Dalkeith
was a family custom later continued at Bowhill.
This photograph was taken before I was born.

Chapter Four

DALKEITH HOUSE AND BOWHILL

B Y TRADITION CHRISTMAS AND NEW Year were celebrated in yet another of our houses, Dalkeith House on the outskirts of the town of Dalkeith near Edinburgh. So it is with Dalkeith that I associate my birthday. After the outbreak of war in 1914 and my grandfather's death, Dalkeith was never to be used by my family again until it was especially opened for the wedding reception of my nephew in 1982. Its treasures were eventually distributed among the other Buccleuch homes and its rooms let out as offices and flats.

Dalkeith, like Drumlanrig, was originally a Douglas stronghold. It had changed hands several times in the course of its history, including a period in the fifteenth century when it acted as the notorious 'Lion's Den' of the Regent Morton, so its stones, though partially reorganised to form an eighteenth-century mansion, have no doubt witnessed plenty of dark and bloody deeds.

It was from the seventh Earl of Morton, a devoted royalist who bankrupted himself on behalf of the king in the Civil War, that my ancestor Francis Scott, second son of the Earl of Buccleuch, bought the property in 1642. Dalkeith has had many royal visitors over the years. James

A Christmas dinner menu at Bowhill. Mr Rowland, the butler, recalls that one year no less than 220 people were given Christmas dinner.

IV stayed there with Margaret Tudor before their marriage in 1502. In 1518 his son James V spent a month there to escape a plague in Edinburgh and held court there in 1526. Charles I stayed for a night in 1633 and in the following century Bonnie Prince Charlie spent several nights despite the fact that his host was a supporter of the Government. George IV came during his triumphant visit to Edinburgh in 1822, Queen Victoria in 1842, and, during my lifetime though I cannot remember the occasions, Edward VII in 1903 and George V in 1911.

General Monk used the house as his headquarters in Scotland during the Commonwealth and is said to have planned the restoration of Charles II from there. The latter, on regaining the throne, married his eldest son — James, Duke of Monmouth — to the Countess Anne Buccleuch. Monmouth was later disgraced and executed for rebelling against his Uncle James II. The eldest son of Monmouth and Duchess Anne did not outlive his mother, so it was their grandson who became the second Duke.

Perhaps it was a murky happening in the distant past of the house that accounted for the spooky spot between the double doors leading into the upstairs drawing-room. Sybil and I had

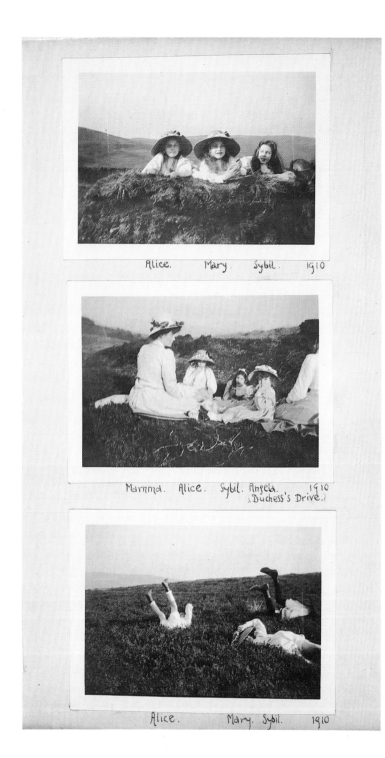

Alice.   Mary.   Sybil.   1910

Mamma. Alice. Sybil. Angela.   1910
(Duchess's Drive.)

Alice.   Mary. Sybil.   1910

*Three young Scotts on a
grouse moor at Langholm.*

to pass there on the way to our mother's sitting-room and always found it an ordeal. We used to hold hands, shut our eyes and run through as fast as possible. Many years later one of my uncles said he felt the same. That was not the only frightening aspect of the place for a child. My Aunt Connie wrote: 'In winter the darkness of the big house scared Francis and myself when the rest of the family was absent. Our quarters were lit, but beyond seemed an endless extent of blackness.' Some of the walls were very deep and the lavatory we used was set into one of these. It was dark and eerie with only one small window for light, high up. We dreaded the door being closed and the possibility of getting locked in. One of the bedrooms had a brass plate on the door inscribed with the name of General Monk; and after the War, when the old cellars were cleared out, eighteen venerable bottles were discovered with a label proclaiming them to be 'General Monck's Amontillado'.

Our journey to Dalkeith was by special train hired to convey the family, servants, carriages, horses, ponies and a vast amount of luggage from Drumlanrig. The Hampdens and other cousins would arrive in due course to swell the numbers. The house was referred to as the 'Palace' by the local townspeople, and contained a great many large rooms with high ceilings and carved doors. The little entrance hall was filled with a huge painting of a Moorish giant. We lived in dread of him coming suddenly to life and springing out to catch us. Beyond lay a long and friendlier hall with a large table running down the middle, covered in tweed coats, capes, mack intoshes, hats, sticks, umbrellas, and more often than not with one or two labradors sprawled underneath. Against one wall stood a splendid weighing machine with

30

Angela and mother sitting for some unknown reason in a patch of burnt heather.

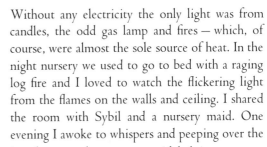

a comfortable leather seat and a place on which to put an array of brass weights, ranging from four stone down to fractions of an ounce. It was a house rule that every guest be weighed when they left and the result written in a visitors' book. Usually facetious comments followed the entries, like 'after lunch' or 'go easy on the pudding next time'. Unfortunate guests of the Buccleuchs had to undergo the same torture at Bowhill, the principle Buccleuch residence in the borders and the house that was later to fulfill the Christmas role of Dalkeith. We loved using the machine, going up and down till the correct number of weights in the balance held us poised.

The large hall was where we congregated for church; the private chapel at Dalkeith was in the park and also served as the town's Episcopalian church. When at Bowhill or Langholm we sometimes used to attend the kirk, so as to offset this Episcopalian preference and show there was no ill-feeling. My mother always professed to be religious but not my father. He attended on Sundays because he felt he ought to, but wound his watch threateningly if the sermon was taking too long. We would complete the poor clergyman's discomfort by running our doormice along the pews. Religion was by no means forced down our throats: in fact it was Sybil who taught me The Lord's Prayer. This was when I was about four. Up until then I could only recite 'Gentle Jesus, meek and mild', which I did not like at all. 'Pity my simplicity', in particular, I found nonsensical and hard to say. Learning The Lord's Prayer came as a great relief. It seemed a very grown-up thing to be able to do.

Without any electricity the only light was from candles, the odd gas lamp and fires — which, of course, were almost the sole source of heat. In the night nursery we used to go to bed with a raging log fire and I loved to watch the flickering light from the flames on the walls and ceiling. I shared the room with Sybil and a nursery maid. One evening I awoke to whispers and peeping over the sheet was much intrigued to see the nursery maid helping a young footman to dry his hair in front of the fire. Footmen powdered their hair before waiting at dinner and were expected to have every trace of it brushed or washed out by the following morning. (Powder was an economy, wigs being more expensive and reserved only for coachmen.) I suspect there was neither hot water nor a warm fire in the footmen's quarters and our nursery maid's friend was luckier than the others, though no doubt he would have got into a lot of trouble had he been caught.

Up in the attics were several enormous trunks full of old clothes: uniforms, crinolines, men's silk embroidered waistcoats and pages' satin suits of pink and blue in a wide variety of sizes. The suits had most probably been made for coronations, but like many of the clothes may have been much older. There were also a lot of smelly old wigs. The clothes dispensed eye-watering wafts of mothballs, but we loved dressing up in them nonetheless. The grown-ups used them as well, donning them every year for a grand fancy-dress Christmas dinner. This traditionally followed a fancy-dress tea for the children. In later years the custom was carried on at Bowhill. It was there that our cousin

Miss Lucy Hope once appeared as a geisha girl. She was a formidable, middle-aged lady with a pronounced moustache and to everyone's horror Billy, the self-appointed master of ceremonies, announced that she had won first prize for coming as an Afghan chief.

When I was five or six I was particularly devoted to my cousin David Brand (later Lord Hampden). One day Billy took us aside and said earnestly; 'If you go into the summer-house in the old wood you'll find a fairy there who'll marry you and let you live happily ever after on Scotch broth and chocolate meringues'. The wood was the remains of the old Caledonian forest of ancient oak trees, a fairy-tale place for all of us children, and at its centre stood an attractive Victorian summer-house, its walls lined with a layer of dry heather and an intricate pattern of fir cones and nuts. David and I followed Billy's instructions and after a prolonged vigil in the hut, during which no fairy appeared, became both disillusioned and frightened. Meanwhile our disappearance had been noticed and the alarm raised: frantic nannies chased everywhere and the river bank was scoured. Eventually Billy was asked where he had last seen us. Following his disclosures we were rescued from the hut.

In one place the river bank was riddled with an eccentric assortment of artificial caves made in Victorian times. One of them was longer than the others and dark in the centre and here we played horrific games of pirates. 'Beetle Juice' was head of the pirates and also had a hide-out in the house — a small, dark room at the bottom of a winding stair, where the footmen cleaned the lamps. Long before I was old enough to be enlisted as a pirate, I was allowed to go and visit this awesome figure, escorted by Sybil. It was quite a while before I discovered that the dreaded 'Beetle Juice' was Billy.

There were plenty of other amusements. In a wide passage on the first floor was a huge grey rocking-horse belonging to the previous generation. Three of us could fit on its back and one on each side of its rockers. Nearby there was a very special grandfather clock. When it struck the hour a row of little soldiers marched past just below the face. 'We used the clock as goal for passage football, or wickets for

An 1812 sketch of Bowhill showing how the architect thought it would look after his alterations.

stump cricket,' writes Aunt Connie. 'It continued to keep perfect time, in spite of bumps and bangs. Now it stands at Bowhill, known to be the work of a famous clock maker, but has ceased its duties as a time-keeper.' Bowhill has another curiosity from Dalkeith: a large case containing a musical box in which, at the turn of a handle, three monkeys in eighteenth-century dress do conjuring tricks on a table with some dice.

Aunt Connie, to whom we were devoted, was a great organiser of games and treats. Before the estate Christmas party she always produced a deep bowl filled with different coloured fruit-drops and these we would scoop, stir energetically and shovel into bags and baskets to hang on the Christmas tree. I always found it rather hard having my birthday on Christmas Day, but it certainly never lessened the excitement and sometimes even had compensations. It enabled me, for instance, to join Aunt Connie on the annual trip to the pantomime in Edinburgh. She referred to it in a letter to me written not long before she died:

> I often think of our pantomime parties from Dalkeith. Mr Whitmore was of the party, as he had charge of the tickets — but why did Canon Cooke go also? Surely a most unsuitable person for a pantomime! I always had charge of the youngest allowed to go, and remember you were allowed to go at an earlier age than others, because of your Christmas birthday. I remember you slept soundly in my arms all the way home in the family bus, and you were quite heavy — but I did not mind as I loved you very much.

The family bus was a horse-drawn waggonette, sitting five aside facing each other. The policies at Dalkeith stood between the North and South Esk. Along the banks were well-kept gravel paths where nannies often took prams and children. When they did so the day before a duck shoot, it caused considerable annoyance to the guns who found all the ducks had flown elsewhere by the appointed time. The head keeper was a splendid fellow called Mr Chowler, who rode about wearing a bowler hat. He was a great expert on the Stock Exchange and visiting guns would buttonhole him throughout the day on the

DALKEITH PALACE,
MID LOTHIAN

subject of their portfolios. Apparently when he died he left several thousand pounds, a lot of money in those days.

One of the most frequent guests outside the family, and certainly our favourite, was my grandfather's friend Lord Rosebery, the former Prime Minister and the last holder of that office to lead in a Derby winner. He enjoyed joking with and teasing us children, and Mary called him 'Lord Strawberry' because of his red nose.

In 1911 my youngest brother George was born in the house just before a visit by King George and Queen Mary. My mother asked the Queen if she would honour the baby by being a godmother, to which she said she would be delighted but she forgot to mention it to the King. The following day the King said to my father that he would like to be the baby's godfather. My father and mother did not dare mention about Queen Mary and gratefully accepted.

The festivities at Dalkeith over, we once again boarded a hired train, just like a circus on the move, and headed for Bowhill at the heart of the Scott country in the borders. The estate lies within the boundaries of the ancient Ettrick Forest — at one time the favourite hunting grounds of the Kings of Scotland. Various Scotts were rangers there in the Middle Ages and, according to legend, it was the courage of a certain young Scott, when saving the king's hounds from a fierce buck deep in a forest 'cleuch' or ravine, that earned the family their titular name of Buccleuch (Buck-cleuch). No part of the eighteenth-century building can be seen by a visitor today, the house having been rebuilt and successively added to during the first half of the nineteenth century.

The new Bowhill was the house most closely associated with Sir Walter Scott. Scott was a kinsman of the family and was befriended early in his career by the third Duke and in his prime by the fourth. Writing in old age of the young fifth Duke, he observed that 'I would not have him quite so soft natured as his grandfather, whose kindness sometimes mastered his excellent understanding. His father had a temper which better jumped with my humour. Enough of ill nature to keep your good nature from being abused is no bad ingredient in their disposition who have favours to bestow.' The fifth Duke proved the match of any that had preceded him, a distinguished public servant and generous private benefactor, who was acknowledged as one of the most enlightened and successful landowners of his time. It was this Duke's

B.Q.   HERMITAGE.

My father walking at Hermitage, Sir Walter
Scott's favourite Border castle.

34

A.C.S.

Lizzie. George. Angela.

mother who gave Scott the idea for his first great literary success 'The Lay of the Last Minstrel' and the poem was dedicated to his father, Duke Charles. The minstrel begins his lay at Newark Castle, a ruin two miles north of the house, and in one stanza refers to the enchantments of 'sweet Bow-hill'.

This is an apt description. Though the house is not beautiful or even particularly distinguished, it was always the happiest and most comfortable of our homes, and placed in a lovely situation between the fast-flowing rivers of Ettrick and Yarrow. In the park and just visible from the windows are two lakes that frequently froze solid in winter, providing a chance for the young to play violent games of ice hockey, and the elderly the more restful sport of curling — their calls of 'Soop! Soop! Soop!' echoing among the hills as they agitatedly swept the ice clean before their gliding stones.

Myself at Dalkeith in 1914 and a later tobogganing picture with Miss Liggins, governess and instigator of our 'schoolroom magazine'.

 Boughton is a mixture of houses and courtyards of varying date. Like many large country seats it was a monastery before the Reformation.

Chapter Five

BOUGHTON

IN TIME FOR EASTER, THE FAMILY WOULD move south again to pass the summer at Boughton, in Northamptonshire. My grandfather handed over this property to my father early in the century, and here, as children, we stayed every year from Easter till the middle of June, when we left for our few weeks as guests of our grandparents at Montagu House.

Boughton, like Montagu House, was originally the property of the Montagu family and became a portion of the Buccleuch estates only when Duke Henry, the third Duke, married the Montagu heiress in the middle of the eighteenth century. The architecture of the house documents the occupations and fortunes of its owners in a remarkable way, from its origins as a monastery, through the homely additions by the knightly Montagus of Elizabethan times, to the Versailles-like façade imposed by the first Duke at the end of the seventeenth century and expressly designed to be fit for a king. He hoped it would tempt William and Mary to come and stay, and thus keep him as much in favour with the Protestant Orange court as the Catholic Stuart one it had replaced. It is, in other words, not one building but a hotch-potch of buildings — its palatial front hiding a positive village of houses and courtyards

We loved Boughton but because it was English we could never admit it.

of varying date, which were best revealed by an aerial view.

However it is Ralph, the first Duke, and John, the second, who have most left their mark. Ralph was in fact born the second son, but his elder brother disgraced himself at Charles II's 76 lines at court by 'squeezing the Queen's hand', and Ralph took his place. In due course he rose to a dukedom and to the post of ambassador at the court of Louis XIV, which experience led him to build this magnificent French château in the heart of the English countryside.

The great north front and many of the treasures in the Buccleuch collections are his legacy, whereas the park is that of his son, John. The latter wanted to have an avenue of trees from Boughton to old Montagu House in Bloomsbury, but was unable to arrange this with the landowners en route. Instead he planted his seventy miles worth of trees in avenues encircling and criss-crossing the estate. Between 1750 and 1900 the house was unused and therefore escaped change to an unusual degree. The only part to suffer was Duke John's elaborate system of canals, lakes and fountains in the park. These have now been dug out and repaired at the instigation of my nephew Johnnie, the present Duke, so that the vista,

HIS GRACE THE DUKE AND DUCHESS OF BUCCLEUCH, BOUGHTON PARK.

enlivened by water effects, is now largely restored to its eighteenth-century glory.

Boughton always reminds me of cuckoos and the cawing of the rooks in the spring and of summer days, warm and peaceful, with cotton frocks (such things as woollen cardigans did not exist then) and wildflowers — bluebells, fritillaries in profusion. We were allowed to roam at large, nobody seeming to worry that we might drown in the lily pond or the river running through the park. We loved the birds and chasing butterflies. We loved Boughton— but because it was English we could never admit it.

Four local villages — Weekley, Walkeden, Ged-

dington and Grafton Underwood — stand at the edge of the park, each a mile or so distant from the house, and on Sundays their intermingling bells made a lovely sound. From each of them, on the first of May, would come in turn separate groups of children, the girls garlanded and the boys holding bunches of spring flowers as they carried their May Queen on a throne smothered in blooms and leafy branches. After singing songs they would dance around the maypole and then, to the delight of all, we showered them with well-polished pennies, thrown as far as possible to cause the greatest chase and scramble.

Cars were a rarity then and bicycling was still a relatively new means of travel. We would often bicycle to Corby, then no more than a hamlet. It was a carefree journey along sleepy country lanes with Corby itself just a single row of houses with one shop, where we would buy sweets before cycling home again. Later it became a steel town and a large number of Scots were imported to man the steelworks. Now that steel has been superceded it has all manner of light industries and today is a New Town boasting a population of 50,000. The idea of letting one of my own grandchildren bicycle from Boughton to any part of it — having to contend as they would with roads and

Sybil. Mary. Alice.

*On warm and peaceful summer days we were
allowed to roam at large in our cotton frocks,
nobody seeming to worry that we might drown
in the lily pond or the river running through
the park.*

RIGHT: Lazing in the park.

RIGHT: An album page of Boughton in 1915, when Walter was back on leave.

Walter. Sybil.   Alice.   Billy   1912.

motorways and hurtling traffic in all directions — would never cross my mind. It is amazing to think that all this has come about within my lifetime.

When it was too wet to be out-of-doors we took ourselves off to the top floor of the house, where endless unoccupied attics were perfect for hide-and-seek. Hardly anyone had been up there for 150 years, and in one room there was a very large and ancient billiard table (revered today as one of the oldest in England), upon which we played many exciting games of our own invention. It was a dusty and mysterious place, and we were forever alert to the possible excitement of meeting the mad Montagu duchess who, according to legend, had been locked up in one of the rooms generations before. She, so the story went, had been a lady of great wealth and equal eccentricity, who declared that the only man she could possibly marry was the Emperor of China. The cunning Duke of Montagu therefore dressed up as the Emperor when he went to ask for her hand in marriage, which of course she bestowed with glee. Then, as soon as the marriage was completed and her wealth secured, he locked her up in one of the rooms in the attic.

The panelled attic walls were painted a pale grey and were full of mice and bats. Bats were a great feature of Boughton. Once, in our absence, some strange noises in my father's sitting-room were investigated, and as a result three hundred dead bats were removed from behind a strip of panelling. Our nursery was a long gallery with a large, carved, wooden fireplace in the centre of one wall, and our schoolroom a beautiful, oak-panelled library of leather-bound books. Most of the rooms in the house were hung with tapestries, one of the Dukes of Montagu having owned the Mortlake factory. To children these could be very frightening as they depicted classical scenes with gruesome animals or violent episodes from the Bible. In a draught they would move gently, which could be alarming in the twilight, and they filled the whole building with a mysterious, peppery smell. Not long ago some rather naughty drawings and remarks were discovered chalked on the wall behind a tapestry in one of the bedrooms. They were the work, apparently, of Sybil and me as children.

The house was cluttered with treasures, but we were never told to be careful of them or anything like that. They were just taken for granted. No curator cared for them, no parties of connoisseurs came to

M.B.Q. George.   Walter.   H.A.S.

BOUGHTON

Walter
on leave from France.
June. 1915.

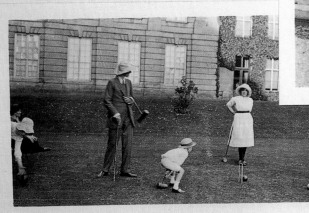

Walter.   George.   Alice.

Walter.   H.A.S.

Aunt Ada's son, Charles, had a motorbike with a wicker side-car. As a special treat, Sybil, then about 13, was allowed to ride it, with me, aged 11, as her passenger.

visit, and my parents were basically uninterested in possessions. My father, it is true, much concerned himself with the pictures, but only in the sense that he liked to see them arranged strictly in accordance with their size. He spent hours with his valet rehanging the collection, but when it came to furniture preferred to sit in the comfort of an old garden wicker chair to anything more elegant. As for sculpture, he and my uncles spent their youth trying to knock the noses off the statues of their Montagu ancestors with cricket balls. The statues stood high off the ground along a colonnade by the front door, so hitting them accurately was quite a test: nevertheless every nose had gone by the time I arrived.

In a distant part of the house lived my Great Aunt Ada, widow of Admiral Lord Charles Scott, captain of the ship in which my father had served as a midshipman. She was a splendid old lady, greatly loved by us all and particularly by my mother. One of her sons, a land agent, lived with her. He had the unique distinction of owning a motorbike with a wicker side-car and, as a special treat, would sometimes allow Sybil, then about thirteen, to ride it, with me, aged eleven, as her passenger. He and his brother, David Scott, flew hawks, which they

kept on hoops on the lawn. The hawks had to be fed live mice and were frequently released to catch small birds. We thought it very cruel but were deeply attached to these cousins nonetheless. David Scott retired to Boughton after a distinguished career in the Diplomatic Service and latterly became a much respected gardener. He died in 1986, just before his hundredth birthday.

Another of our favourites was Great Aunt Ada's niece, Maie Ryan, who occasionally appeared from Australia. Her future husband was to become Lord Casey, Governor of Bengal and later Governor-General of Australia. She was always spirited and entertaining and was still flying an aeroplane in the 1980s at the age of ninety.

The summer of 1914 found my eldest sister Mida grown up, Walter (Lord Whitchester) at Oxford and Billy at Sandhurst. At Montagu House there were dinner parties for the young and Mida's coming out ball. Sybil and I would leave our beds and peer out of the window to watch the assembled guests sitting or walking about on the terrace below. Occasionally we would shout a rude remark to some special friend or drop a message or vulgar drawing. Now and again Walter arrived in the schoolroom with a party of Oxford friends;

Prince Paul of Serbia, an Oxford friend of my brother Walter, was a frequent visitor.

Boughton. 1919.

Mary.

pillow fights and much teasing and ragging were the inevitable result. More often than not he would be accompanied by 'Bobbity' Cranbourne (the late Lord Salisbury), Mike and Rose Bowes-Lyon, (brother and elder sister of the Queen Mother), Prince Paul of Serbia and a young German, Count von Beiberstein. The schoolroom would be left in chaos, our governess, few of whom lasted more than a year (not surprisingly), having tactfully withdrawn. The Great War was about to break out, irrevocably changing the lives of us all.

My grandfather outlived my grandmother by two years and died that first autumn of the war. He was buried at Dalkeith. When we heard we were going to the funeral we felt grand and grown up but also terrified that we might see his corpse. This we were spared, but on the day I was no less horrified by the sight of the coffin being lowered into the vault. I do not think children should be made to attend funerals. Afterwards a period of mourning was observed during which we were all plunged into black, even to the buttons on the footmen's livery.

The Library.

Miss Alice.

The Third Form.

St JAMES'S

1917

Jean.   Diana.

Miss Arnold. Griselda. Diana.

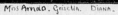

Miss Alice. Miss Di.

Chapter Six

PARENTS AND SCHOOL

Y FATHER, BEING THE SECOND SON, HAD NEVER expected to succeed to the title. He was educated at the Royal Naval College, Dartmouth, and would have been destined for a brilliant career in the navy had his elder brother not unexpectedly died in a shooting accident. At the age of twelve as a midshipman he went on a two year cruise to Australia and the Far East in the *Bacchante*, commanded by my great uncle, Lord Charles Scott. The ship was a corvette of 4,000 tons, fully rigged but with auxiliary engines. Also on board as naval cadets were the two sons of the Prince of Wales — the Duke of Clarence and Prince George, later to be George V. They were accompanied by their tutor, the Reverend John Dalton. As a result of this long voyage, King George and my father remained always the closest of friends. Mr Dalton afterwards submitted an exhaustive log of their experiences to Queen Victoria, which shows that the cruise was not without its perils. A seaman fell to his death in the South Atlantic and between South Africa and Australia they ran into a tremendous gale. The sails were reduced to tatters, the rudder was half wrenched off and for three days the ship drifted out of contact with the rest of the squadron, 400 miles from the nearest port. Eventually sufficient repairs were made to bring the ship to safety.

What was not mentioned in the log was the happy incident when Lord Charles assembled the ship's company before docking at Sydney, and warned them about the many attractive girls they might find there and the importance of not succumbing to their charms. In the event, it was

LEFT: St James's School at West Malvern was run by two of the Miss Bairds. Five spinster sisters all destined to be Head Mistresses, the Miss Bairds were very tall. It was said that laid end to end they measured a cricket pitch.

none other than Lord Charles himself who succumbed to the charms of an Australian girl, Ada Ryan, whom he subsequently married. News of this supposedly inferior match was received with horror back home, but my family need not have worried. Aunt Ada proved a great addition, as I have already indicated. She was a charming and delightful person and lived to be ninety-five, loved by one and all.

My father was still only in his twenties when in 1886 his elder brother slipped on a wet rock at Achnacarry while out stalking. His rifle went off and severed the artery in his arm, with the result that he bled to death before his companions could get him off the hill. Accordingly my father had to leave the navy, much to his sorrow, and return home to shoulder the responsibilities of an heir, which included, in due course, taking a bride. I suspect my two grandmothers arranged the match between them. They were both members of the Court: my father's mother being Mistress of the Robes to Queen Alexandra and my mother's mother, the Countess of Bradford, lady-in-waiting to the future Queen Mary, then Duchess of York. They knew each other well and were the best of friends. Soon after my father's return two Bradford daughters barely out of the schoolroom, the beautiful Lady Beatrice and Lady Margaret Bridgeman, were dispatched to Drumlanrig.

It is difficult to imagine anyone less well prepared for marriage than my mother must have been, after her secluded upbringing at her country home in Shropshire. Her father, by all accounts, was inconsiderately mean towards his family and interested only in racing and his own health — for the benefit of which he made

Guida – short for Granny Ida – was my maternal grandmother. Here she is photographed on the staircase at Drumlanrig.

frequent visits to the spas and resorts made fashionable by the Prince of Wales, leaving my grandmother with virtually no money and six children to bring up.

To us 'Guida' (short for Granny Ida) always seemed rather serious and reserved, even something of a goody goody, but my husband told me that in his childhood 'Ida B', as they called her, had been a great favourite with him and his brothers and sister, very much the life and soul of the party. The spark remained, as is well illustrated by the fact that she was the first person to fly with the Prince of Wales after he received his licence, though she must have been in her eighties at the time.

My other grandmother, Louisa, Duchess of Buccleuch, was also greatly loved and much respected at Court. She had a host of friends as well as a large family to entertain, something she thoroughly enjoyed. A daughter of the Duke and Duchess of Abercorn, she was the eldest in a family of thirteen, which enabled my father to have two uncles younger than himself. Many years later, at a lunch party when my son William was about six years old, the conversation turned to the subject of large and small families and I casually remarked that my grandmother was one of thirteen. I saw William looking horrified and when the guests had left he asked me if what I said was really true. 'Of course,' I replied. 'But how dreadful!' He exclaimed. 'Did they have to drown some?' The labrador had just had a litter of eleven pups, five of which had had to be drowned, doubtless causing him much distress.

I do not know how long my parents' courtship lasted. They were both very shy so it may have taken some while. My mother told me that one Sunday, when my father was staying at her home, Weston, Guida told her firmly, 'You're starting a cold. You'd better not go to church.' Mamma, always meek and mild, agreed, though she had not the slightest symptom of a cold. My father then said, 'Oh well, I'll stay and keep you company.' By the time the church party returned they were engaged.

In due course they got married. It was brave of my mother to accept the proposal. She was only eighteen and, for someone who had never been away from home, it must have been quite alarming to join such a large and boisterous family. As it was, I do not think she ever really blossomed. My father always liked noisy, cheerful people; but my mother found it difficult to compete with social gatherings. We did not see much of her but when we did she nearly always seemed to be lying on the sofa or on a long-chair in the garden. When my father invited his noisy ladies to stay — Lady Mabel Howard, who never stopped talking, or our Aunt Celia Scarborough — she generally disappeared to bed with a 'headache'. Her main interest was in her babies, with the boys always favourites. Having babies also gave her an excuse, I am sure, to get away from everyone — this enormous, tiresome, family of quarrelsome Scotts, her noisy brood of little girls driving her mad! Her favourite child was my youngest brother, George, who was a dear little boy; luckily he grew up none the worse for it.

Her somewhat sparse education had been shared with three sisters

My mother at Boughton with my younger sister Angela.

and given by an elderly governess. She had little idea of how to run a house or who was supposed to do what, so left everything to the housekeeper. Housemaids living in freezing cold rooms in the attics — that sort of thing — simply did not enter her domain. My sister-in-law Rachel Scott remembers her visiting Bowhill towards the end of her life and being excited to discover it had a basement. Where she thought the food had been cooked is hard to imagine. And yet she would often take the remains of the roly-poly pudding, or something equally unsuitable, to old ladies in cottages on the estate who probably did not want it a bit.

I always felt sorry for my mother, even when I was a child. My father seemed continually to be away and she can scarcely have known anyone outside her family before marrying him. The visits she made with us children to Hyde Park, wearing the extraordinary hats she made herself, to be waited on by her collection of funny old gentlemen seem, in retrospect, all the more pathetic and sad. She must often have felt very lonely.

My father also hated formal events, but was sociable enough in his own house. He enjoyed arguments and political and historical discussion, voluble men and talkative ladies. He was never at a loss for a word and usually the winner of any argument but was kindness itself beneath it all.

What he most despised was any kind of pretension. Asked to open some event at the New Club in Edinburgh, he agreed only when he was convinced there would be no pompous ceremony involved. Arriving in Princes Street on the day, however, he spied from a distance that the Lord Provost and city fathers who were lined up outside the building waiting for him, were all dressed up to the nines. So he told his chauffeur to pull up the Rolls Royce at the tram stop, got out and, to the astonishment of the dignitaries, arrived at the Club stepping off a tram.

He disliked his tea being too hot, and at functions always delighted in practising his usual habit of sloshing it from cup to saucer and back to cup again; no doubt some snobs foolishly imitated him thinking this was the ducal way to do it. At home the valet would pour my father's tea about five minutes before he appeared for 9 a.m. breakfast. Nervous young men would come down, see this cup waiting to be drunk, and think, 'I suppose I'd better take it', only to be mortified a

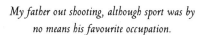

My father out shooting, although sport was by no means his favourite occupation.

few minutes later by my father furiously deman-ding to know where his tea had gone.

Breakfast was also the cause of a rift between my father and Lord Frederick Hamilton, one of the two uncles younger than himself. Getting to the dining-room rather punctually one morning, Uncle Freddie devoured my father's boiled egg as well as his own. As this took place in the middle of the war at a time of considerable food shortages, one egg represented a fair proportion of the official weekly ration. My father was furious and banned him from the house forthwith. But Uncle Freddie was too much of a favourite of us all for the order to hold for more than a week or two. He was full of fun and jokes at mealtime — usually rather vulgar ones delivered in a loud voice, which made the footmen giggle.

After the war my father's dining-room troubles were still not at an end. He was particularly pained by the way Lady Victoria Manners hacked the ham, and it became the custom to hide it during her visit. At Langholm the place chosen was under the typewriter in the secretary's room next to the dining-room. The poor lady must have had some awful shocks as she settled to the afternoon's work!

The war ended and meals returned to their pre-war scale. At breakfast, apart from the array of dishes on the hot-plate of porridge, eggs and bacon, kidneys, sausages, mushrooms and toma-toes, there would be a ham, a tongue and, in the appropriate season, a choice of cold game. On top of lunch and tea, there were enormous dinners of soup, fish, entrée, roast, sweet, savoury, cheese and fruit, with a different wine for every course. Rowland our head steward, who had joined the staff as schoolroom footman in 1915, remembers a good deal of entertaining going on even during the war. He soon rose to the rank of butler and later on, steward. According to his account the total staff at the new London house, 2 Grosvenor Place, consisted of a steward, a housekeeper, a valet, an under-butler, two parlourmaids, five housemaids, a cook, three kitchen-maids, two still-room maids, two ladies-maids, two odd-job men, a carpenter, a steward's room boy, two nurses, a head

FROM MY BEDROOM WINDOW AT 2 GROSVENOR PLACE

The road outside Grosvenor Place was sharply uphill. I would often wake to the shouts of the carters and the merciless crack of their whips as the dray horses struggled to Covent Garden market.

coachman, a second coachman, a carriage groom, three stablemen and a chauffeur. Breakfast in the steward's room was regularly composed of beer and cold mutton. Doubtless more than half the food sent to the dining-room returned uneaten downstairs to the benefit of those below.

Miss Barford was our governess when the news was broken that Sybil and I were to be sent away to boarding school. This came as quite a shock. I was twelve and a half, Sybil fifteen. Mary, Angela and George were in or about to come into the schoolroom and I suppose, if we had stayed at home, it would have meant employing a second governess. Heathfield was the most fashionable school of the time and the one to which my mother had originally thought of sending us; but when she saw what she considered to be the unnecessary and unsuitable lavishness of its clothes list — white silk frocks, white silk stockings, white satin pumps for dancing class — she

Villa St. James's. 1919.

dismissed it as a possibility. In contrast, St James's, the school chosen, called only for white cotton shirts and navy blue coats and skirts.

The school was at West Malvern, Worcestershire. It was an unusual Victorian house built by Lord Howard de Walden on the slopes of the Malvern Hills. It had a lovely view and was surrounded by beautiful grounds and gardens, tended by a school of lady gardeners. Miss Alice Baird had charge of the Senior House and Miss Diana Baird, her sister, of the Junior House of eleven to fourteen year olds. The Miss Bairds were remarkable — five spinster sisters all destined to be Head Mistresses and all very tall. It was said that laid end to end they measured a cricket pitch.

The journey to school was a great adventure for us. We travelled alone, usually breaking the journey to stay a night with our grandmother, 'Guida', at Castle Bromwich, an Elizabethan manor that still stands, but is now lost in one of the busiest areas of Birmingham. Then it was

Billy on leave in July 1915. Both my brothers fought in the trenches during the First World War and were fortunate enough to return unscathed.

Billy   on leave.   July. 1915.

surrounded by beautiful gardens stretching away to a golf course and small aerodrome. To add to the enjoyment of our train journeys Sybil and I used to take a little cardboard box with a hole in it; when anyone opened the door to come into the carriage, one of us would say nervously to the other, 'I do hope the bees don't escape!' That usually made sure we didn't have any company.

Although I was under age, I was allowed to join the Senior School at St James's, so as to share a sister's room with Sybil. Four little rooms were set aside for this purpose at the far end of the house, necessitating a lot of running to and from the main scene of events, but having the advantage of being distant from all its noise and clatter. The Miss Bairds did their best to make school life as pleasant as possible, but

nevertheless it was something of a shock after the comforts I was used to at home.

The position of the house was exposed and it could be bitterly cold, especially in our bedroom annexe, with its three outside walls and windows to the floor. Even in winter these windows had to be opened at night and sometimes we would wake to find snow on the floor. It was cold in the classrooms, too, because of the war-time shortages, which also affected the quality of the food. Main meals seemed to consist of nothing but rissoles, and I broke a tooth on a nail in my porridge. My brothers were even worse off at the Front. They wrote continually of food. A letter from Billy in the summer of 1915 is typical:

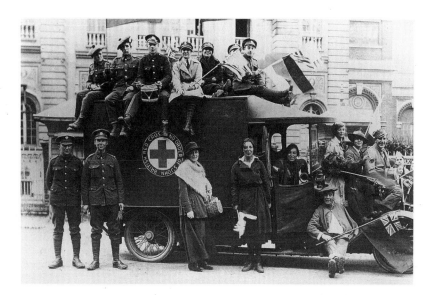

Armistice Day 1918. Being that bit older, my sister Mida played a more active role in the War than I.

Dear Alice,

You might let my father know that several articles arrived safely, viz, 1 Fowl in tin; 2 tins of sardines; 3 tins of herrings; 1 tin of rolled ox tongue; many tins of cream, cocoa etc, also such items as Dubbin.

We live entirely on the tinned stuff from England as the only meat out here is pork and the ration beef is not very tempting.

The asparagus is very good: but the best of all was the fowl in a tin.

What I particularly want is a tinned ham, or a big corned beef to have as a midday meal, and some salad oil or mayonnaise sauce would be very useful.

Cakes are also very useful. In fact send the same as now only more.

We have had a quiet time in the trenches with only a few casualties.

I am only about 12–16 miles from Walter but cannot arrange to see him.

Love from Billy.

Letters were a rarity in the Second World War, everything being so heavily censored, whereas in the First World War everything was quite open. After lunch Miss Baird would read us newspapers reports of the fighting. The death lists, which covered all ranks, were a daily horror, but nevertheless we were not unduly anxious.

It all seemed very far away from St James's. My parents never wrote and no relatives came to visit us during our time there — we were more than thankful, for we felt sure they would have disgraced us by saying or doing the wrong thing!

Being philosophical, we realised we had to be at school, so had better make the most of it and enjoy everything there was to enjoy. I was soon enrolled as a Girl Guide, which I took very seriously, continuing my connection with the Movement for many years afterwards. During what I presume must have been an epidemic of the often fatal Spanish flu I was more or less in charge, only five of us out of both pupils and staff remaining unaffected. When you are young and healthy such crises only add to the excitement and adventure of life and I coped well enough. I also greatly enjoyed the games and had no difficulty with the lessons. On arrival I had been placed in a class of girls a year older than myself but never found any trouble keeping up.

There were no 'O Levels' or 'A Levels' in those days, and exams were not taken seriously. 'Citizenship' was what the Miss Bairds were most anxious to instill and it must be admitted that they did so with considerable success — many girls were later notable for lives of public service. In my time there were about eighty pupils, but I did not make any great friends. People never seem to do so at school.

 I joined the Girl Guides when I was at St James's and played an active part in the movement for many years.

A Concert in the Barn.

FANCY DRESS SUPPER.

E. PATROL

 A Girl Guide camping trip on the coast in Fife.

A Langholm family portrait taken by my great
uncle, Lord Ernest Hamilton. He asked us to
'look our best' — this was the result. I am
second from the right.

Chapter Seven

LANGHOLM

BOARDING SCHOOL CERTAINLY MADE US MORE APPRECI-ative of home, the joy of the holidays amply compensating for all the boredom of the long and seemingly endless terms. Bowhill and Drumlanrig served as hospitals from the outset of the war, which meant that we spent Christmas and Easter at Boughton — where we were entertained by a regiment of Scottish Horse encamped in the park — and August and September at the Lodge, Langholm.

Up till that time only male members of the family had gone to Langholm since it was used exclusively as a shooting lodge, but now that it had to serve as a holiday house we all crammed in. The building consisted of a large dining-room and drawing-room and many small bedrooms, with an additional 'tin hut' at the back, containing four bedrooms and a bathroom, where younger members of the party were quartered if necessary. Except for the small town of Langholm with its wool and tweed mills, there was nothing but moorland for miles around. Langholm was a real holiday house and for that reason the one we most looked forward to visiting. It was the same with the older generation. Uncle George remembers a grouse shoot when the enthusiasm of guns and beaters was such that they managed to fit thirteen drives into a single day.

Grouse abounded in their thousands, so officers on leave were welcome to come and shoot. Most keepers and estate workers had left to join the army, so Sybil and I were commandeered to beat and load, each being given a wise old labrador for picking up the birds. Mine was called Alice, which seemed rather a mistake! Luckily she made it slightly less confusing by only answering to 'Ulus'. During a day's shooting one walked miles, struggling in and out of peat hags and trudging through heather as high as one's knees. Maybe it was this that made me such an indefatigable walker forever after. There was an unusual number of grouse during those war years. On one occasion, when loading for an elderly 'crack-shot', I marked down the positions of over eighty fallen birds at a single drive on the back of an envelope.

Andrew Smith, the head keeper, was our guide and master, a well-respected figure in the neighbourhood and lifelong friend of many of the guests who came to stay over the years. His wife was a wonderful cook and many were the memorable tea-parties we enjoyed in their cottage.

There were three fell ponies at Langholm called the 'Black'un', 'Brune'un' and 'Grey'un', which were used to carry the hampers of dead game and sometimes to provide a lift for old or infirm guests, who found the walking too tiring. On non-shooting days Andrew Smith, who was a knowledgeable naturalist, used to lead us out riding on these animals. Often such expeditions would last the day, during which we would probably call in on one or other of the tenant farmers scattered around the estate. They and their wives would give us a warm welcome and something good to eat and drink.

One day the 'Black'un', to receive his carrot, suddenly jumped the railing round his paddock with the ease of a roe deer. 'How splendid!' exclaimed Mary, 'Now we can take him hunting!' And, in the years following the war when the hunt was again in full swing, I would ride him regularly late in the season up in the hill country he knew so well. He loved it as much as I did, never tiring or refusing a jump or stumbling over the 'sheep-drains' which abounded on that difficult

THE Lodge

September
1917.

George.

Uncle Francis.

Mary.

ground. He instinctively recognised bogs, stopping to paw the ground and snort so as to let me know to give him his head and find his own way round. Often we would end up the day deep in the moors twelve or more miles from home, with me quite lost; but I always knew that with a loose rein he would unerringly find the way back without a moment of hesitation. Out of season he lived at Bowhill where he pulled the mowing machine or took household washing to and from Selkirk. He was a truly remarkable animal and lived to a good old age of thirty or more.

One of the great joys of Langholm was the annual gymkhana, which took place every September. An anonymous account of it in our 'magazine' may lack polish but catches the spirit of those carefree days very well.

This was perhaps one of the chief events of the season this year, and spectators flocked from all parts to see some remarkable and entertaining equestrian feats of varied and amusing description.

The races took place on some suitable ground behind The Lodge and opened at a quarter to three. The day was August 23rd, Friday, a beautiful sunshiney day.

A large audience assembled on the course amongst whom were Lady Ewart and Miss Ewart, Sister and a large number of wounded soldiers.

Eight horses were proudly paraded before their admiring gaze by a bevy of smart grooms.

Stella, Dale, Biddy, Smith's Brown Mare, the Black'un, Lewis, Grey'un and the Brun need no further description in this account, as all readers are fully acquainted with their various points and habits and peculiarities. Competitors for the Gymkana comprised the Ladies Sybil, Alice, Mary and Angela Scott; Lord George Scott, Smith, Mr Read, Mr Simson, Charlie and Reggie and Mr Behrens. The Reverend R. Hodge and Mr Walter Forbes Esq. were acting as judges.

The opening race was a fast race all round the field at the back of the house. The ponies displayed their best paces and their mettle in it, and were stimulated to greater efforts by the encouraging cheers of excited spectators.

In the Cigarette and Umbrella race, Lady Alice came in first, triumphantly waving an unfurled

Summer holidays at Langholm. George is on Merrylegs and Mary on the Black'un.

umbrella to an excited audience and puffing out clouds of cigarette smoke in their delighted faces.

She further pleased them by falling off the Black'un in the Bareback Race — it was remarked that an expression of relief immediately came over its face just as though a heavy load had been taken from its mind!

Charlie won the Threadneedle Race on Black'un, his needle being threaded by the Duchess, for which he carried off a box of toffee while the Duchess received a photo frame. Whether it contains Charlie's photo or not has not yet been ascertained but there is no reason for its not doing so in the future, when Clarke carries off the Cup in the Grand National.

Reggie won the Bareback race and bore off in triumph a fine portrait of the Duke. The Dress up Race was one of the attractions of the day. It was won by Smith who careered nobly into the winning post clad in strange raiment. But even a dressing gown and black hat could not disguise his fine and noble form, bursting with perfect health and fitness and looking not a whit the worse for food rations. He fully deserved the valuable prize — in the shape of a handsome pincushion – which was awarded. At five o'clock the programme came to an end and all flocked off in search of refreshment.

After tea a game of rounders was played with the soldiers. One distinguished himself by hitting a ball over the house to the astonishment and pain of Mr Read, whose head broke its fall and whose fall nearly broke his head. It is a tender spot with him to this day.

Another event which deserves some mention was Mrs Ewart's unwitting interpretation of doing the Cinderella stunt! At least she lost her heel, which mishap brought her into close contact with terra firma. Her feelings were much hurt, especially when she viewed the hole caused by her fall. Visitors, newly returned from France, have since mistaken it for a shell hole and have to be enlightened. Jack Ewart, a most promising young gentleman among the guests, threw a ball with such vigour that the sheep whose head received it has since died of an apoplectic fit.

Everyone remarked upon the excellent quality of the mutton next day, while Jack proudly exhibited his prize, which he has embellished with some deer's horns as one of the trophies of his deer stalking in the highlands this summer! We know better who killed Mary's little lamb. Jack?

At 7 o'clock the brake carried off the the

reluctant wounded and the sister to the hospital. Only one incident marred their joy ride back. It was a minor one, but the wheel of the vehicle came off. Fortunately for her but hardly for her victim, Sister landed safely and gently on Scotty's head. We are relieved to be able to add before this goes to Press, he will be convalescent for a few days; as the services of a famous surgeon whose name is so well known that it is superfluous to put it here — otherwise known as the Face Repairer were requisitioned immediately. He proudly declares it to be one of his most difficult and successful cases.

So ended happily a long remembered and never-to-be-forgotten day in the annals of LANGHOLM.

I suppose hunting was my favourite sport but fishing ran it a close second and never more so than at Langholm. Sea trout fishing tends to take place at night, and that I loved best of all. The fisherman stood silently behind, ready to disentangle my fly if it caught in a tree (or his cap) and to remove it from the jaws of the fish when caught — an operation I could never bear to perform. While we floundered along the river bank between pools, he would inform me of local gossip. I

should have preferred silence, with the occasional hoot of an owl, but did not like to tell him so. Some of the fishing was several miles downstream towards the Solway, which necessitated a drive home in the dog-cart pulled by one of his ponies. Clip-clopping along the empty road, moonlight shining through the larch trees on either side, I felt this was a perfect end to the day — particularly if a basketful of trout was coming home with us.

Andrew Smith never allowed us an idle moment. 'If it's too wet to shoot it's no' too wet to fish!' he would announce when it rained. For his own private war against the foxes he kept two huge deer hounds. One day the cook at Langholm, Mrs MacDonald, left a leg of mutton on the window-sill. 'Algy', one of these pets, got wind of the morsel and made off with it. Later she broached the subject with Andrew. 'Dinna fash yersel woman,' he said. 'It'll no' do him a bit of harm'.

Another occupation supervised by Andrew when it was not a shooting day was to take us out on to the hill to pick sphagnum moss as part of the war effort. We would collect it in sacks, and then lay it across the lawn on dust sheets to dry. Afterwards all the bits of heather and peat, dead frogs and other foreign bodies had to be picked out

Jan.   Saucy.   George

BELOW: My father with Andrew Smith, the head keeper. The latter never allowed us an idle moment; 'If it's too wet to shoot it is no' too wet to fish!'

before it could be sent to the hospital. There it was used instead of cotton wool for swabbing out wounds as it was a good disinfectant being full of iodine.

Close to Langholm was the Solway Firth and along with all the fun of the sea there were also its perils. When I was about fourteen my mother took the younger children to a place called Seascale on the Cumberland shore of the Solway. Mary and I lost no time in putting on our bathing things and scampering down to the beach. The tide was out as far it would go and the two of us walked and walked in about a foot of water. At last it got a little deeper so I said, 'I'll go till I'm up to my waist and then you swim out to me.' I could not swim very well and Mary was just learning but on I went when suddenly a wave came. I found myself up to my neck, then out of my depth. I shouted to Mary to go back, but she

Papa. Smith.   1912

had not come as far as I had and had already turned back and was splashing for shore.

I swam and swam, but it was no good. Whenever I searched with my toes for the bottom there was a frightening void. I guessed I was in the grip of a current. Apparently there had been a sign warning of this danger on the beach but in our excitement we had not noticed it. My mother was alone and as she came on to the beach she saw this sign and to her horror spotted us far out. Some women passed by and, distraught, she asked them to help. They said they could not see what they could do. In the meantime I began to feel too tired to go on and thought, I'll drown and be done with it. So I gave up, and as soon as I did the shock of the water closing over me brought me to my senses. I thought, I don't want to die! I'm so young. Surely I'm too young to die now! I've hardly had any life. And I prayed Oh God,

Seascale. Sept. 1918.

GEORGE. MARY. ANGELA.

George Rosemary Lottie.

*Seascale on the Cumberland shore of the Solway
Firth. It was here in 1914 that I was almost
carried out to sea.*

give me my life and I promise I'll make use of it if you'll give it back to me. Almost immediately my toes touched rocks and in a minute I had struggled to my feet and was able to stand up and get my breath back. I had been carried quite a way — some distant houses had come and gone I remember — and was still far from the shore but the rocks proved to be a reef which carried me back to the shallow water without further mishap.

My mother was furious. 'How could you do such a foolish thing! You might have drowned your sister as well as yourself! I've never had such a fright!' and so on, which was not very comforting; nor was there any need for it. The incident had changed my life. For years it haunted me. I had made a covenant: in return for my life I felt I must dedicate it to some superior and useful purpose; but there never seemed to be anything that required my help or that I was particularly good at. So

Langholm.
1916.

61

when, through a series of unforeseen events, I one day found myself allotted a life of public duty in

A later picture of my sister Mary with her husband, David Burghley, the Olympic champion.

the service of my country, for me a very special pledge was honoured.

OUR
MAGAZINE

Sunday Morning at Langholm

As girls we amused ourselves, like so many families at the time, by making our own magazine, encouraged by Miss Liggins, our governess (right). Nowadays the young, alas, watch television instead.

Our Magazine.

2.

Contents.

DECEMBER.

OUR MAGAZINE

ACMDS. 30.3.16

The magazines were monthly with covers to match. Miss Liggins' Schoolroom Alphabet makes fun of the War but, with two of our brothers at the Front, this was doubtless to raise our spirits.

Schoolroom Alphabet.

A for our Army, the nation's delight.
All praise to the boys' who've gone out to fight.

B for the Belgians who've suffered so much,
And bore it like heroes; we treat them as such.

C for Canaries, the family of Sweeties -
Their singing and chirruping to hear such a treat is!

D is for David, a dashing young brass hat
Who sits out all the dances & sprawls on the doormat.

E for Edith the nursery maid, parlourmaid too.
They both ought to be in a cage at the Zoo!

F for Frankie Lloyd with his corsets so tight.
He never removes them not even at night.

G for small Georgie, our brother so good,
Or at least so he might be, supposing he could!

H for the Huns we despise & detest.
They've already found out they will never have rest.

I for the Irish renowned for their wit.
If they'd help with these rhymes, they'd be doing their bit.

J for the Jumpers that Sybil displays -
To admiring admirers who continue to gaze.

K for King's Guards - no ladies allowed there
Since tiresome Dick Sheppard conveyed such a crowd there.

L is for our Lift which sometimes wont stop.
If you get in at the bottom, you get out at the top.

M Is for Mother. To please her we try.
We dont always succeed but cannot tell why.

N for the Navy afloat or ashore,
Lads in blue jackets whom all girls adore.

O for Our readers - you'll come from near & far
We hope, to enjoy the Babies' Bazaar.

P for Prince Paul, Archie's dear friend,
What if their friendship should suddenly end!

Q for Queenie Manners - a talented lady
She laps up the cream which was meant for the Baby.

R for Compt de Rhybes to Boughton he came
All thanks to our pedigree as well as our name.

S for Sir Everard, the best of old friends
How good are the chocolates he so seldom sends.

T is for Tony, the writer of verses,
Not much of a suballern, he gets many curses.

U for Utopia - now that women have votes
They expect to achieve one - alas for their hopes!

V for Vacani whose wonderful dancing
Starts us hopping & skipping & jumping & prancing.

W for Walter who makes us more cheerful.
From morning till night - no time to be tearful

X is an Xercise hard for my mind
I cant find a word, please forget & be kind.

Y for your Yawns as you read o'er these rhymes
Dont get too downhearted, this year of hard times

Z for the Zeppelins 'Let them all come' we say
But their dear fatherland will mourn them next day.

E.M.L

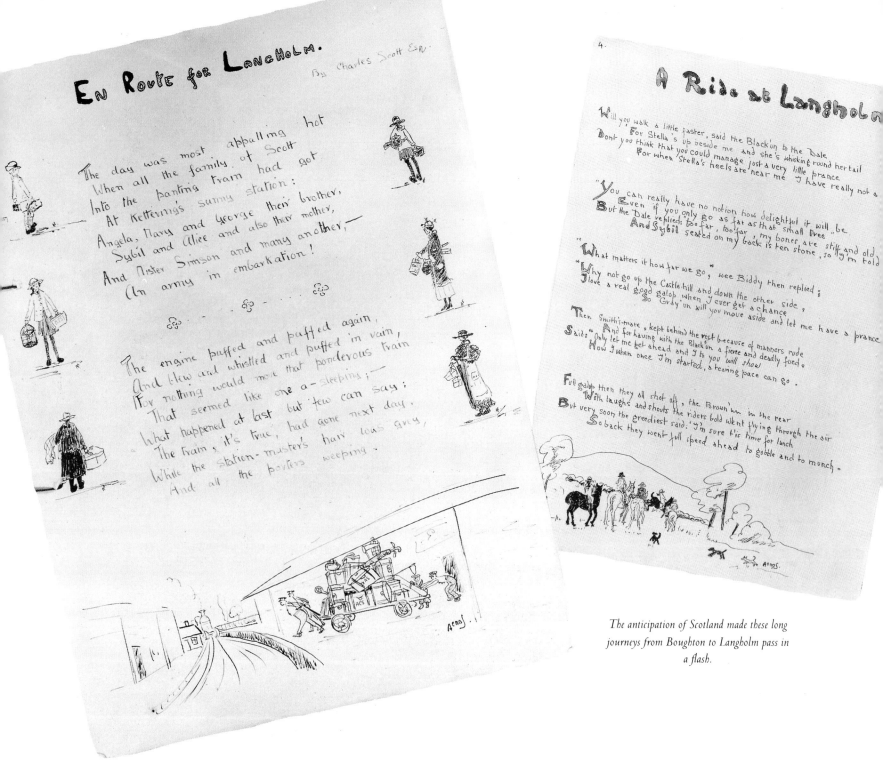

En Route for Langholm.

By Charles Scott Esq.

The day was most appalling hot
When all the family of Scott
Into the panting train had got
At Kettering's sunny station :
Angela, Mary and George their brother,
Sybil and Alice and also their mother,
And Mister Simson and many another,—
An army in embarkation !

The engine puffed and puffed again,
And blew and whistled and puffed in vain,
For nothing would move that ponderous train
That seemed like one a-sleeping ;—
What happened at last but few can say :
The train, it's true, had gone next day,
While the station-master's hair was grey,
And all the porters weeping.

A Ride at Langholm

"Will you walk a little faster, said the Black'un to the Dale,
For Stella's up beside me and she's whisking round her tail
Don't you think that you could manage just a very little prance
For when Stella's heels are near me I have really not a

"You can really have no notion how delightful it will be
Even if you only go as far as that small tree"
But the Dale replied: "too far, too far, my bones are stiff and old
And Sybil seated on my back is ten stone, so I'm told

"What matters it how far we go", wee Biddy then replied ;
"Why not go up the Castle-hill and down the other side ,
I love a real good galop when I ever get a chance
So Grey 'un will you move aside and let me have a prance

Then Smith's-mare, kept behind the rest because of manners rude
And for having with the Black'un a fierce and deadly feud
Said: "Only let me get ahead and I to you will show
How I when once I'm started, a tearing pace can go.

Full galop then they all shot off, the Brown'un in the rear
With laughs and shouts the riders bold went flying through the air
But very soon the greediest said: "I'm sure t'is time for lunch
So back they went full speed ahead to gobble and to munch.

*The anticipation of Scotland made these long
journeys from Boughton to Langholm pass in
a flash.*

THE DUCHESS OF MONTAGU'S BALL

News of the Month.

By Lady A. Scott.

APRIL.

1. Lord George carries on a campagne for making people April fools from 7. A.M to 12. A.M.
2. Prince Paul arrives at Bowhill. No one can stop yawning!
3. " " amuses himself by throwing stones through the drawing room window.
4. Easter Sunday. We all descend upon St Mary's, Melrose, to hear Mrs Lockton sing in the choir.
5. Strange looking sausage appears for breakfast, and is devoured eagerly by P. Paul.
6. Prince Paul has a slight attack of rabies and bites Aunt Ada when she comes to call.
7. Point-to-point Races. Everyone backs "Fauldshope". Consequently are badly down, at the end of the day.
8. Lord Dalkeith sends his hat to the village band, to be used as a concertina.
9. We visit the Gray Mare's Tail. Lady Margaret & Miss Liggins partake of a showerbath by sitting under it.
10. Last Meet of the Season at Bowhill. Aunt Ada & Coolin get persued along Duchess's drive by hounds.
11. Furniture-Van is hired to take Lady Margaret's London hats to the station.
12. The family emigrate to 2 Grosvenor Place. Train is very exhausted when arrives St Pancras
13. Great preparations for Devonshire House Ball. The Duchess, Lady M. & Lady A. try on numerous wigs.
14. Day of Ball arives! Lady A's fancy-dress is discovered to be too tight. Luckily one remaining hook & eye [stays on too]
15. Lady Alice attemps to wash her hair. The powder in it turns to photo paste! [Up twilt p. eggs]
16. Three bad plovers' eggs for lunch. Several people faint. For future occasions, gas masks are to be brought
17. Miss Warrender comes to tea. She must have slipped in through the letter box.
18. We all go to hear Lord William's sermon to the "Purity League" at the Marble Arch.
19. Mrs Sweetie meditates building a nest.
20. She starts it, by pulling out several long hairs from Miss Liggins best coiffure, while snoozing on the [sofa]

21. Lady Margaret & Lady Alice stay with the Dean for a dance at Windsor Castle.
22. Lord Dalkeith decides to go to Canada. Weeping and gnashing of teeth amongst his lady friends
23. Lord George is run over by a bus but and comes up unhurt the other side. [on the doorstep]
24. Lady Alice & Lady Mary go on a visit to Chalcot. Edith welcomes them with a beaming smile [one of Lady A's hens]
25. Lady A. & Lady M. are conducted round the domain by Lady Sybil and Mr Phipps. Lady A. gets badly pecked by
26. They leave Chalcot. Lady Mary is accompanied by a large flee given her as a keepsake by one of the hens
27. "Three-legs" is lost. Two clefftectives are telephoned for. They hunt for Three-legs' footprints [not in use]
28. "Threelegs" is found. Nestling amongst Lady Margaret's false curls. Which she keeps in a box when [not in use]
29. The first strawberries appear ∴ George has a billious attack.
30. Shops are very crowded owing to the number of people buying parting gifts for Lord Dalkeith

Doings of the Season.

Baby Angela has 13 teeth out.

Miss L. gets run over in Piccadilly by the Landau.
The Epitaph is extraordinarily appropriate "Nothing in her life became
her life the leaving of it." No flowers by request.

*Miss Liggins caricatures the ups
and downs of a governess's life
while Sybil, by now out of the
schoolroom, dreams of
trousseaus.*

ANGELA or the SWIMMING BATHS.

SHALLOW END

E.M.L.

Her Motto:. I ought. I must. I will. I can!

58.

A bed-jacket of blue trible-ninon edged with white fur. Motifs of old lace are let in on the shoulders and a bow of ribbon fastens in front. The couvre-lit is of pale pink satin turned back with fine white linen across which, meanders motifs of lace. threaded with ribbon. A broad flounce of lace edges the coverlet, as also the pillow made to match.

This attractive Breakfast jacket is of flesh pink chiffon, round in shape. It is bordered by a deep flounce of Malines lace. The coverlet & one pillow is of blue satin, with inset bands of Filet lace, bound & lined with Old rose The other pillow has a lattice pattern of lace, & a large ribbon bow.

An evening frock for a flapper is made in white net, with a tunic of white Georgette held in place by a sash of ribbon brocade.

A loose and comfortable dinner gown after a hard days sports or play in soft white chameuse. The sash is of deep rose-coloured chiffon, & the skirt slopes over a petticoat of the same.

RUTHLESS RHYMES.

By Lady Alice Scott

Simson playing golf one day
Hit the ball to his dismay
Right through the eye of Harold Potter
Who turned & said: "you are a rotter!"

Angela in sunday hat
Tripped & fell on front door mat
With piece of string across the hall
That rascal George had caused her fall!

There was a young lady called Mida
Who found in her pudding a spider
With a flick from her hand
She soon made it land
Down the neck of the person beside her.

Billy of the 10th Hussars.
Though he'd like to visit Mars.
When he got there — Oh how sad!
All the Plovers eggs were bad.

Mary Theresa Montagu Scott
Before going to school discovered a spot
So great was her joy and huge was her glee
Tho' really she knew t'was haughty but a flee

She scratched & picked till it was red;
The docter came and shook his head,
By my grey and grizzly locks
"I swear it is the Chicken-Pox!"

Walter is a Guardsman gay —
Who frequently at dance and play
Is seen beside a lady fair
With eyes of blue and fluffy hair.

SEEN IN THE PARK

"Bonjoor, Mademoiselle"

Society Snapshots, Things We Want To Know and News of the Month were all inspired by features in the London Mail, *a gossipy newspaper of the time.*

Things We Want To Know.

Does Mrs Paterson make the gooseberry skins (that are thrown over her wall) into Jam?

What did Mr Hodge say when he found that Uluse had eaten up his breakfast?

Has anyone noticed the extraordinary likeness between ladies Alice and the Brow'un?

What is the quarret between the Black'un and the brown mare?

D. Scott.

How long will it be before the Scott Eliots call here?

Where do the Scott Elliots get their petrol from?

Who will be the first person to drown in Dowie?

How long will it be before all the gooseberries in the garden are gone?

Who will ride Stella in the bare-back race, in the Gymkarner next month?

Which swims the fastest, Rosie's puppy or Sybil?

Why is it that Alice frighten all the fish so, when she bathes in the river?

Which is the fattest? Alice or the Grey'un? Why are they so alike?

PART TWO

The Twenties

David Brand.   M·I·S· Paul Bridgeman. M·B·Q· Victor Cazalet. Alice.   April. 1920.
Fancy-dress Ball.   Devonshire House.

*A fancy dress ball at Devonshire House in April
1920. Our magazine records: 'Day of Ball
arrives! Lady A's fancy dress is discovered to be
too tight. Luckily one remaining hook and eye.'*

Chapter Eight

COMING OUT

WHEN PEACE WAS DECLARED IN 1918 I WAS still at St James's, but left soon after to attend finishing school at Neuilly on the outskirts of Paris. Here, two charming sisters of the French mistress of St James's ran an establishment for the benefit of eight girls of similar age to myself. We were a happy party and some of us remained friends for many years after. I think I am the only one still alive. We were supposed to improve our French and were not allowed to speak English. Cooking and dressmaking were part of our curriculum; the rest of the time we went sightseeing, being taken as a special treat to the opera or ballet. I saw Pavlova in Swan Lake and was lastingly impressed. The only disagreeable aspect of these outings was the journey on the Métro — the reek of garlic among the pushing crowds I found quite nauseating. Apart from having accompanied my mother on one occasion when she took the waters at Aix-les-Bains, this was my first stay abroad.

My future sisters-in-law, Molly Lascelles and Elizabeth Lyon.

Mollie Lascelles   Elizabeth Lyon.

RIGHT: The three princes arriving for the service.

BELOW RIGHT: The wedding of my brother Walter and Molly Lascelles in April 1921, with myself as bridesmaid.

April 21st 1921

After several months of this delightful existence with the Mesdemoiselles Delpierre in the rue Charles Laffitte, I returned to England, supposedly ready to burst forth into the world of debutantes and coming-out dances. By 1916 we had moved into 2 Grosvenor Place. My father never much enjoyed London life and staying at Grosvenor Place, but he found it quite convenient for visits to the House of Lords and for watching cricket. He seldom went to a club and was apt to sit for hours by a downstairs window at home, playing patience between working on the speeches he was always being called upon to deliver. One day, passing on a bus, I overheard two young men in front of me betting each other as to whether or not 'the old bloke' would be in the window playing patience. Sure enough, there he was.

Sybil was now married to her dashing cavalry officer Charles Phipps, and gone off to live in Wiltshire. I missed her and all the fun she brought with her many young friends, who greatly enlivened the rather quiet and melancholy atmosphere of our new London home.

Very shy and rather plump, I made a miserable début at a dance at Windsor for Princess Mary's birthday, uncomfortably squeezed into a white satin frock. Prince Henry was ill at the time and had to miss the occasion, not that I noticed. I was far too preoccupied with my own anxieties, and spent most of the evening behind a pillar.

Attendance at endless deb dances ensued. I thought them dreadful. There was always a chaperone, if not one's mother then one's maid, who had to wait in the cloakroom. The degree to which one had to be chaperoned knew scarcely any bounds. Some cousins, the Lovelaces, lived

Mothers usually accompanied their daughters to dances. The girls would be handed a dance card, which they often filled in with a lot of bogus names, in case some old bore came up searching for a partner.

just around the corner from us in London, but even for their tea-parties we had to be dropped and picked up by a maid. The footman would spoil the fun with his dread announcement of her arrival. *Thés dansants* — with cakes, tea and lemonade for refreshment — were popular during the war while rationing still applied.

Mothers usually accompanied their daughters to dances. The girls would be handed a dance-card, which they often filled in with a lot of bogus names to make it look as if they were booked up in case someone boring came along searching for a partner. It was difficult to say 'no dances left', because they would insist on asking while looking over one's shoulder. When a little older and more cunning and experienced, we would make daring unchaperoned escapes to a night-club. The opportunity for this arose when elderly gentlemen, who seemed to exist solely for this function, gathered up the mothers and took them off to supper or the bridge-room. In this interlude one could be away from the party without much chance of being missed. I never really enjoyed the nightclub once I got there but was too polite to admit it. I did not drink or smoke and never have to this day, I danced round and round or sat silently at a table, then insisted I had to

go — perhaps rather earlier than necessary — on the pretext that the parents' supper would soon be over. After a year or two I refused to go to dances unless I knew some of my special friends would be there.

Being presented at Court was somewhat alarming. In my debutante days, one was still required to wear a train and three mysteriously symbolic feathers in one's hair.

When we left school each of us girls was given an annual allowance of £200, paid into our bank accounts in quarterly instalments. We lived at home and an allowance was not expected to cover anything much apart from clothes. Entertainment and travelling costs were never a consideration; tips when one stayed away as a guest were distributed by one's maid, who was then refunded by the house steward. A housemaid could expect to receive a tip of five shillings. Dresses were hideous — very short and straight with a belt around the hips. Sleeves went out of fashion. A young French friend once staying for a Hunt Ball was discovered to have cut off the sleeves of all her evening dresses to accord with the prevailing taste and had guiltily hidden them away at the back of a drawer in her dressing table. Her mother must have been horrified.

ARUNDEL

JUNE
27 ⤳ 29.

DUCHESS OF NORFOLK.
BERNARD. RACHEL
LADY DRUMMOND.
MARGARET.
COL & MRS M. DRUMMOND
MYRA

MR GUINNESS
DERICK HOYER MILLAR
GERALD MAXWELL
MARY MAXWELL
MR TUFTON
ULICK VERNEY.

*ABOVE: Country-house parties spent with the
Norfolk family at Arundel were particularly
happy. We stayed at Ramslade (opposite) with
Sir Everard Doyle, one of my mother's admirers,
when he took it for Ascot.*

RAMSLADE. JUNE 16-25

ASCOT
ROYAL ENCLOSURE
1923

The Lady Alice Scott

COWES.
1925.

SHAMROCK.   LULWORTH

Mr PEDLEY. Lord HINCHINGBROKE. Mr JEFFRYS. JOHN MONTAGU.

SHAMROCK.

*During Cowes week I once stayed with the
Montagus at Beaulieu. The towers of Beaulieu
can be seen in the background of my sketch
(bottom left).*

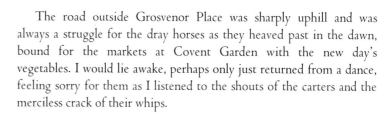

The major events of the season — Ascot, Wimbledon, Goodwood — were much as they are today, though Wimbledon then had only two courts. After the war ended, my Grandfather's tradition of taking a box at Lord's was resumed. For the two days of the school match enough lunch for 150 guests, many of them ravenous schoolboys, was packed in ice caves and transported daily to the ground. On these occasions the kitchen-maids had to be up by about 4 a.m. to hack the ice blocks with pickaxes so that the caves could be bedded in at least one hundredweight of ice chips for the journey. An ice man delivered blocks to the house twice a day. In hot weather ice could be consumed at a rate of ten hundredweight in a week. The first sitting of the Lord's lunch was for Eton boys their own. When they left they were each tipped a pound by my father.

My life, as that of my friends, was principally devoted to pleasure, but in so doing we meant and, I think, did no harm to anybody. Summers in particular were a succession of country-house parties and ones spent with the Norfolk family at Arundel and Kinharvie, their Scottish home in Dumfriesshire, were particularly happy. Life in London filled the gaps between the house parties.

The road outside Grosvenor Place was sharply uphill and was always a struggle for the dray horses as they heaved past in the dawn, bound for the markets at Covent Garden with the new day's vegetables. I would lie awake, perhaps only just returned from a dance, feeling sorry for them as I listened to the shouts of the carters and the merciless crack of their whips.

DRUMLANRIG
AUGUST.
29

ARTHUR COOK. ANGELA. TEDDYBROOK. MARY. GEOFFREY BRIDGEMAN.

A.C. ACRS. T.B. MTS. AS.

A Twenties house party at Drumlanrig.

82

Chapter Nine

THE TWENTIES

For me the early twenties were a relaxed an carefree time. At Bowhill during the winter months hunting provided my main occupation and source of exhilaration. I possessed only one horse of my own, but fortunately my brothers were kind enough to lend me theirs should they have one spare. For two seasons I was lent a lovely thoroughbred by a friend who had to go abroad with his regiment, so, what with the addition of an occasional mount on one of the hunt horses, I did not do too badly and managed two, if not three, hunts a week. I thought of little else, which seems strange to me now but gives me sympathy for those many young people who enjoy this particular sport. There is, I have found, much one can learn from it that is helpful in everyday life: endurance, quickness and perception, speed of decision, 'give and take', infinite patience and tolerance from handling horses, as well as 'bump of locality' and sense of direction. The latter was to be particularly helpful to me at a later date in East Africa.

The Buccleuch Hunt covered an extensive area and its followers were apt to come out only when the meet happened to be within reach of where they lived, so there were never the large

Prince Henry, Philip Donna and my brother Billy at a Border meet. They were fellow officers in the cavalry and Billy often brought Prince Henry to stay when they were both on leave.

crowds that often spoil the fun of hunting in the Midlands. I knew everyone by sight and name and a friendly crowd they were; most of them belonging to families who had farmed, lived and hunted there for generations.

In those days when leave from the army was fairly easily obtained, Billy would frequently arrive home for sporting weekends accompanied by brother officers including, on occasions, my future husband. Contact with Prince Henry was not confined to these hunting and shooting parties at Bowhill or Drumlanrig because, when the regiment was stationed within reach of London, he was also a frequent visitor to Grosvenor Place. He was expected to stay at Buckingham Palace if he was passing a night in London, but this necessitated his saying exactly where he was going and what he was doing; so his use of our house was kept a secret, even from my parents. In fact only Rowland, our head steward, would know the exact arrangements. Billy and Prince Henry used to arrive late in the evening, change, go out to their party, return for a few hours' sleep and leave by seven to be on parade by eight. The family were usually in bed before and after they had come and gone and so remained unaware of their visit.

WATTIE SCOTT. AS. BUSTER FINDLAY

FAR RIGHT: When frost made the ground too hard for hunting, we organised paperchases through the woods or ice hockey. In those days it seemed to freeze almost every year.

ABOVE: My winters were given over to hunting and house parties in the Borders.

Cavalry officers from the regiment stationed in Edinburgh would keep their horses at the stables in St Boswells and come and hunt at the weekends, often staying with us at Bowhill. Amongst them were Charles and Elspeth Miller, destined to join us during our stay in Australia as private secretary and lady-in-waiting. Others, alas, were victims of the Second World War, notably Ranulph Twistleton-Wykeham-Fiennes, father of the explorer. A younger hunt follower, whose future one could hardly have foretold, was a small plump boy on an even plumper pony led on a rein by a large Mama on a vast horse. This was Willie Whitelaw. His father had been killed in the First War and his widowed mother came to live in the borders. His grandfather, who lived in Edinburgh, was one of my father's greatest friends.

Another enthusiastic member of the hunt was Earl Haig, the Field Marshal. I often found myself riding alongside him on the way back to the kennels where my horse was kept. His home at Bemersyde was a few miles farther, on the same road. He was a delightful and friendly person and his daughters were our closest friends. When frost made

the ground too hard for hunting, we and the young Haigs would organise paper-chases through the woods or mixed ice-hockey matches. Once we even played the 13/18 Hussars at their barracks just outside Edinburgh. The matches were always furious and fast and on this occasion Doria Haig broke a bone in her ankle. On our return home Lord Haig was most annoyed and asked why on earth the referee had let things get so out of hand. We then had to admit that there had not been a referee. This made him even more angry, but in the end all was forgiven.

After Doria Haig's wedding to my cousin Andrew Scott, we had a picnic on the road home, by the Grey Mare's Tail Waterfall in Dumfriesshire. It was a famous beauty spot, and when we came screaming down the hill dressed in our wedding finery, the men all in top hats and tail coats, a party of sightseers gave one look and rushed in terror for the safety of their charabanc.

Like myself, Xandra, another of the Haig daughters, helped with the Girl Guides and one summer her troop from Roxburghshire joined

ON THE PIER AT BLACKPOOL.

On the pier at Blackpool. We must have been staying at Teddy Brook's shooting lodge on the Lancashire moors.

with mine from Selkirk at the same camp. Most inconsiderately she brought her father's camp-bed, a very grand iron affair weighing a ton. It would not fit into any tent so in the end had to stick out into the field. It was the only bed we had and could not have been more of a nuisance. The camp itself, however, was a great success. The Guides all cried the first night because they were homesick and again on the last night because they did not want to go back!

By the time I was grown-up cars were fairly commonplace. Most of them were open, with hoods that went up when needed. When we grew older my sisters and I were given a Morris Cowley to share between us. Cars had balloon tyres at that date — if anything pricked them they burst — and one day as the three of us were merrily spinning along to Edinburgh that is exactly what happened. I found myself standing

My father's caterpillar car. He liked to frighten guests by taking them up and down the precipitous banks on the estate.

in a field of turnips. Mary emerged out of the ditch at the other side of the road, but where was Angela? After much agitated searching we discovered her underneath a bramble bush. She proved to be the only one of us that was hurt — her collar-bone was broken. After a lift home from a kindly passing motorist; we left her in hospital with everything duly taken care of. Mary and I took the plunge and broke the news to my father. He was wrestling with *The Times* crossword, and did not look up while we nervously awaited his reaction. There was a long silence. 'What's a three letter word for sheep?' he asked. 'Ewe?' we suggested. And that was that.

One of my father's greatest sources of pleasure was his caterpillar car. This was a sort of small open tank with caterpillar tracks instead of wheels. There was virtually nowhere it could not go and we travelled in it together around the

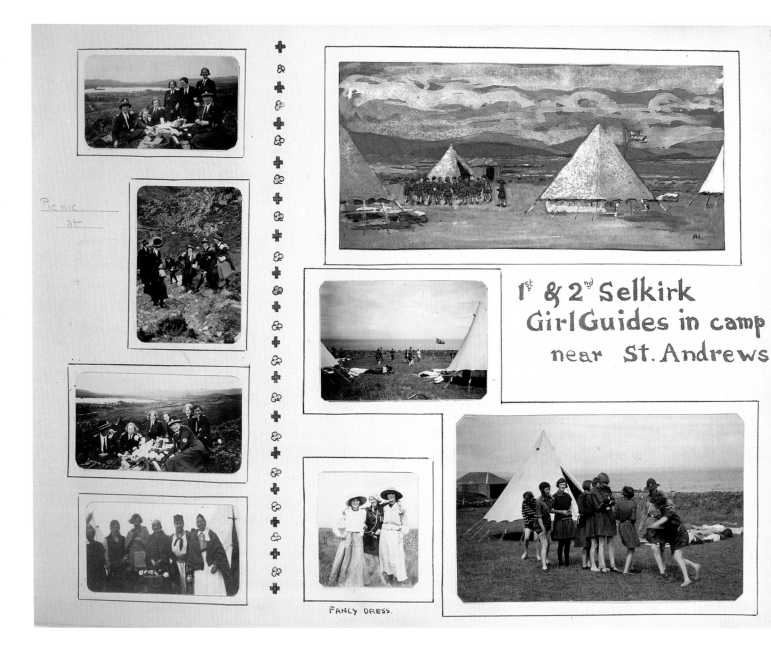

Picnic
at

1st & 2nd Selkirk
GirlGuides in camp
near St.Andrews

FANCY DRESS.

*Camping with my Girl Guide group from
Selkirk. My friend Xandra Haig brought her
father the field marshal's camp bed, an enormous
iron affair which stuck out of the tent.*

Hotel St. Georges.

*At the Hotel St Georges,
Algiers, April 1924. My trip
there with Sybil, while she
was convalescing from flu,
was my first glimpse
of Africa.*

woods and farms. He liked nothing better than to frighten the wits out of unsuspecting guests by taking them for drives up and down the most precipitous banks on the estate. He got the idea of having one of these machines from the Duke of Beaufort, who used his for following the hounds.

We were easily and innocently amused by today's standards: acting and paper games, the various forms of hide-and-seek, and more energetic favourites like billiard fives and 'Frieda', which entailed tearing round the billiard-table at great speed. Practical jokes were also considered extremely funny. These took numerous forms, from simple apple-pie beds to more complicated tortures, usually reserved for pompous young men. We would stitch mustard plasters in the seat of their evening trousers and watch them suffer agonies at dinner. It was this sort of behaviour that made Prince Henry so much appreciate life with the Scotts. He was treated just like everyone else. My mother insisted on rolling out a red carpet for him when he arrived, but the rest of us ridiculed this and I think he found it an embarrassment. No fuss was made of him otherwise, and to me at first he was significant only as one of the more regular visitors from among my brother Billy's

regimental friends — a shy, unassuming young man who was always happy to join in the fun.

In April 1924 I had my first glimpse of Africa. Sybil had had a bad attack of influenza and her doctors advised her to take a recuperative holiday in the sun, so she decided she would like to visit North Africa. She was married by then but nothing would induce her husband to accompany her — he was busy with their farm in Wiltshire and anyway hated going abroad — so it was planned that I and a mutual friend of ours, Nellie Baillie-Hamilton, would come along instead. Finally, an admirer of Sybil's, a staid and very proper gentleman called Colonel Southey, said he would like to come too, and as he had a large car we all decided this would be a good idea. The party was completed by a rather ancient lady's maid, who also acted as Nellie's chaperone. With the Colonel at the wheel we set off for Algeria.

It proved a happy tour with beautiful scenery and warm sun, and certainly did the trick as far as Sybil's health was concerned. Nellie was a great character, whose spirits and good humour never flagged. She ragged poor Colonel Southey mercilessly, upsetting him by pretending to have fallen madly in love with some undesirable sheik, from whose

At Biskra an old man told
my fortune by making marks
in the sand: 'I see a crown
and much to do with the
army. You will travel many
long distances.'

Colonel Southey.   ACS.   Sybil.   Tata Waw.   Nellie.   de Bourréal.

ALGIERS.
APRIL.
1924.

clutches it seemed that the Colonel would imminently have to rescue her. He bore it all very well. For me a memorable moment in the adventure took place at the oasis town of Biskra. Here there was an old divina who told our fortunes by making marks in the sand. When it came to my turn, he took a long while and then said in French that I would marry someone of higher station than myself. Since I was a Duke's daughter this seemed rather unlikely to me. But he insisted, 'I see a crown and much to do with the army. You will travel greatly, many long distances.' I thought this all sounded nonsense.

Mr Rowland was now established as head steward of the Buccleuch household. According to his written account, every day at 7.30 a.m. he would go through the house we happened to be in at the time, seeing that all was in order. Then, after his breakfast at 8.30, he checked all the clocks to see that they were telling the correct time and settled down to his routine cellar or office work. Running the household was still a massive enterprise. Untold tons of logs and three to four hundred tons of coke and coal were alone used every year in fuelling it. Christmas at Bowhill continued to be as much of a feast as at Dalkeith. The festivities lasted a month, with an average of eighty mouths to be fed at every meal. One year no fewer than 220 people were given Christmas dinner. The standard order was for 150 lbs of turkey. The business of moving from one house to another was miraculously completed in a matter of two days. This included the transport of 250 pieces of luggage, collectively weighing no less than eight tons.

Delivering food from the kitchens to the dining-room along the endless passages at Drumlanrig required split-second timing if soufflés were not to fall flat or the weekly haunch of roasted venison arrive stone cold. Once a footman took a wrong turning and got lost in the house with the second course for dinner. Even guests could go astray, especially after the port and cigars. To prevent this there was a red line painted along the passage wall to indicate the route between the smoking-or billiard-room, in a remote wing of the Castle, and the

(PASSING GUANO ISLANDS!!!)

A.C.S.

We passed these islands when with the Athlones in South Africa. The smell will remain with me forever.

main building. It was considered bad form to smoke when the ladies of the house might be around, so the gentlemen were given this special room well out of smelling distance.

The cellars at Bowhill and Drumlanrig each contained two 54-gallon barrels of whisky — the equivalent of 100 dozen bottles — which were never allowed to be more than half empty, and there were similar supplies of sherry and port. All of this and much more was the responsibility of the steward. It is easy to see why the stock response to every problem was, 'I'll ask Mr Rowland.'

This watchword was used to ultimate effect one morning when my father asked a footman if it was raining. 'I'll ask Mr Rowland, Your Grace,' came the reply. My father summoned Rowland. 'Has that footman any brains at all?' he said. 'If he had any more he would not be here,' answered Rowland. My father frequently closeted himself with Rowland after dinner, to discuss family matters and current events quite as much as the problems of the household. Sometimes they talked till the early hours of the morning, my father pacing up and down as if he was back on the deck of a ship. Rowland was no less a confidante of ours. It was not done to have drinks before dinner in the way that it is now, at least my father would not allow it, so Rowland used to supply my brothers and their friends with a tipple in the steward's room at 6.30. Only my mother noticed. 'Why, I wonder, does Billy always have to see Rowland every evening?' she puzzled. But, of course, his secret was secure.

In 1926 I went again to Africa but this time to the Cape. The Earl of Athlone was Governor-General of South Africa at the time and my elder sister Mida was lady-in-waiting to his wife, Princess Alice. When she got engaged to Commander Geoffrey Hawkins, ADC to the Governor-General, it was decided that it was more convenient to hold the wedding out there.

South Africa in those days offered no hint of future disharmony. It seemed the most blissfully happy place. One never saw a glum face. Perhaps the most memorable expedition in which I took part was a shooting safari in Zululand. This took place during an Easter holiday for the staff. We took no tents, and our entire equipment was put on a wagon and drawn by twelve donkeys. One morning at crack of dawn the others all went off to shoot rhino. Princess Alice had allowed me to go only on condition that I did not take part in the shooting of this particularly dangerous animal, so honouring my promise to her I stayed and tidied up at camp with the Africans. Suddenly there was not a soul to be seen, the Africans were all huddled under the wagon. Glancing round I saw mother rhino and her baby trotting down towards us. I hid under one of the camp-beds, praying she would not scent me, and to my great relief she passed by. The hunters later returned, exhausted and empty-handed, having not seen a rhino all day. Afterwards I wished I had been bolder and taken a photograph.

On another occasion Sir Richard and Lady Howard Vyse — Sir Richard was nicknamed 'Wombat' because of his resemblance to that

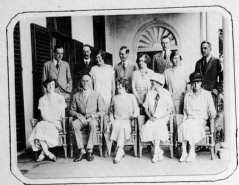

GEOFFREY. UNCLE HARRY. KAITLIN. CECIL. A.S. JOHN. MAY. REGGIE.
MIDA.　　H.E.　　MAMMA.　　H.R.H.　　"WAGS".

KAITLIN DAWSON. IRIS TAYLOR.
MAY CAMBRIDGE. A.S.

GOVERNMENT

HOUSE.

CAPE TOWN.

ABOVE: *Cape Town 1926, staying with the*
Athlone's at Government House for the wedding
of Mida to Geoffrey Hawkins, their ADC.

OPPOSITE: *Afterwards I went to Zululand and*
to the Victoria Falls.

90

ORCHARD.

animal — arrived at Government House in the course of their honeymoon. Unwisely they mentioned that their next stop was Victoria Falls. 'Oh, Alice hasn't seen Victoria Falls,' said Princess Alice forcefully. 'You'd better take her along with you!' The last thing they can have wanted was company, but they obligingly agreed and off I went, with Mida's enormously fat maid to look after me. Needless to say they could not have been more welcoming and indeed protective. When they went to see me safely on to the sleeper for Natal to visit Uncle Harry Bridgeman, Hermione Vyse was put out to find that my maid had been consigned to a different part of the train. 'Who's next door to Lady Alice Scott?' she demanded. It turned out to be Ivor Guest, later Lord Wimborne, a young man whom I knew vaguely from England. Hermione confronted him immediately. 'You can't possibly be next to Alice Scott,' she explained briskly, 'You must move to another carriage. Her maid has got to go in here.' The disgruntled young man was put to flight. We subsequently met on many occasions and I am glad to say he bore me no malice.

South Africa was idyllic, but its legacy turned out to be a frightening bout of cerebral malaria. One morning I woke up with a mosquito bite on my elbow. Apparently the train I was on had stopped overnight in a cerebral malarial district, but not knowing this at the time I thought no more of the bite till, crossing the Equator on the homeward voyage, I developed a fever and soon fell unconscious. It was a horrid experience. In delirium I thought I was a tree in a tin. All my limbs were growing and I could not get them out, so that the more they grew the more they ached. Luckily, the greatest living authority

A RIDE IN A RICKSHAW AT BULAWAYO

HUGH. HARRY

MARGOT. SIBELL. P.HENRY   PATSEY.   P.D.   HARRY. HUGH GWEN.

A Boughton house party,
Easter 1928. The oarsman
is Prince Henry.

on tropical diseases, Dr Rabagliate, happened to be on board, and one of the passengers had some dope that pulled me through, but I was lucky not to die.

I convalesced at Boughton. Nothing could have been more of a tonic. After dinner, we and our guests would go out into the woods to hear the singing of the nightingales. It usually ended — at least for the younger members of the house party — with a rough and tumble in the bushes. Another pastime I especially associate with Boughton, though we played it as fervently at other house parties, is treasure hunting. This involved going off in pairs — a boy and a girl — after dinner, with a list of about twenty items that had to be collected as soon as possible from the surrounding countryside. Whoever arrived home first with their full consignment were declared the winners. Inevitably there were silly things to be fetched, like Mrs Corrigan's stays, or ones that involved dare-devil 'burglaries' on neighbouring country houses, perhaps obliging the hunters to motor twenty miles or more. It was great fun for us, but must at times have been very irritating for other people. It was a great age for after-dinner games and we would often settle down to charades, or some sort of paper game like consequences.

At the time, I remember some of the responses people invented seemed very daring, but I am afraid the young today would think them boringly innocent.

Our most intriguing neighbour at Boughton was probably Mr Brudenell of Deene, who wore a square top hat and long cloth cloak indoors to keep out the draught. I first met him when I was about fourteen. My mother had announced, 'We must have the new owner of Deene Park over for lunch. I believe he's stone-deaf so we'll have to shout.' On the appointed day my mother duly shouted at Mr Brudenell through half the meal and then, turning to Mida, said 'Your turn now.' Mida took over the shouting and after lunch we all shouted 'goodbye' to him. A few weeks' later at a flower show, I was again introduced to Mr Brudenell. 'Ah yes,' he said, 'you and your sisters made rude remarks about me all through lunch. I can lip read, you know!'

Another time at Boughton my father had a professor of forestry over from Cambridge for lunch. Afterwards they toured the woods with the retired head forester, Mr Neill. When the tour was over my father turned to Mr Neill and said, 'Well, have you learnt anything from the professor?' 'Not a damn bit! It was all a lot of rot!' he replied.

Elizabeth Lyon.   Katharine McEwen

 Elizabeth Lyon and Katharine McEwen staying
at Bisham, a house that Captain and Lady Nina
Balfour used to take in the summer.

ABBEYSTEAD.

July. 28 - 30.

LONDON   GREYSTOKE

Lady Mabel Howard.
Lady Carnarvon
Lady Clinton
John Harrison
Lady E. MacDonnell

GREYSTOKE

July. 30th
August. 2nd
1921.

NEWTON DON.
NOVEMBER. 1928.

LEFT: Aurea Balfour at Newton Don, a house of many happy memories.

The embarrassed professor then left. 'Neill,' said my father, 'you should not have said that to the professor... but I must admit I do agree with you.'

A delightful friend of both my father and mother was Lady Mabel Howard. She often came to stay and regaled us with amusing stories. She drove herself, most dangerously and usually on the wrong side of the road, in an aged Morris Oxford. The car was named 'The Humble One' and was well-known wherever it went — most people stopped and got as far off the road as possible when they saw it coming. My sister and I quite often stayed with her at Greystoke Castle. We always enjoyed going there, in spite of it being haunted and creepy at night, with no electric light, badly fitting windows and doors that creaked and banged. Lady Mabel lived on her own but asked endless guests of all ages, who were welcome at any time. She would always arrange amusing expeditions for us and it was never less than the greatest fun to be with her. We all loved her dearly, as did many in the county of Cumberland and the town of Carlisle, where she did endless good work for the benefit of the needy.

Her sister, Lady Nina Balfour, another particular favourite of my father's, was one of our neighbours, presiding at Newton Don in the borders. She was also a great character and an incorrigible matchmaker, which was rather off-putting, but there was no hostess in Scotland who could equal the deliciousness of her food, her impeccable taste and flair for a party. She also had a rollicking sense of humour. One of her favourite jokes concerned one of the many balls at Newton Don, and an elderly waiter who had been engaged to do the formal announcement of the guests. He was not very experienced at the job and shortly after the start of the presentations he was flummoxed by the arrival of two horse-drawn buses from which large numbers of people descended. He correctly gauged that this was the Duke of Roxburghe and his party, but despairing of their numbers, proceeded to announce them collectively as 'The Party from Floors'. Then, met by a wave of arrivals from the second bus, he bellowed, 'And some mair of 'em!'

Aunt Celia, Countess of Scarborough, was another of my father's favourites. She was not always popular, because she would insist on attending the grouse shoots carrying a yellow umbrella. If it started to rain in the middle of a drive — as it usually seemed to — up went the

I joined the Selkirk branch of the Red Cross and went on to become a VAD.

umbrella and all the grouse flew into the next county. I think my father rather encouraged her because it made all his relations, who took shooting a great deal more seriously than he did, beside themselves with rage. My mother was not interested in the shooting, but she was subtle in showing her disapproval. She just pretended she could not tell the difference between one bird and another. It was a fiction she kept up till the end of her life. My brother William and his wife Rachel were once staying at Branxholm, the home of her old age, and Rachel remembers her saying to the cook, 'Lord William will have a cold wing of snipe for breakfast.' A snipe is, of course, about the size of a sparrow.

An aunt who made a great impression on me was my mother's youngest sister Helena, Lady Sefton. The other Bridgeman aunts and my mother tended to be rather prim, but Aunt Nellie could not have been more forthright or spirited. Long before the First World War, she shocked her relations by wearing trousers and going off big-game shooting with a boyfriend — needless to say, it was the trousers that caused the worst scandal. In the last War she drove lorries, though by then she was well over seventy. She was terrifically given to good works and a very religious person. I was very impressed when she once took

me down to the canteen in the docks where she often helped cook breakfast for the merchant seamen who had come in the night before or at dawn.

Possessed as I was by a strong sense that I ought to be doing something to help others, I went one night a week to help the captain of the Selkirk Guides and Rangers, and also joined the Selkirk branch of the Red Cross, eventually becoming a VAD. My mother disapproved of this, thinking it wrong and dangerous that I should drive myself to and from Selkirk — four miles distant — alone and after dark through the winter months. She would probably have been even more disapproving if she had known that on the way home I invariably gave a lift to old Tom the odd-job man, who regularly walked to the town in all weathers for a drink at the pub.

Some of my happiest memories from this period are of skiing at St Moritz in January of 1927 and 1929. How very different St Moritz was in those days to the crowded resort it has become. The few people who did go were mostly English and American. I went out with the Haddingtons, Xandra Haig and Sarah Haddington's sister Dorothy. Being Canadian Sarah and Dorothy were both expert skiers and

SUVRETTA HOUSE

St·Moritz

Betty Cranborne

A.S. Geordie Haddington. Xandra Haig. Gaspard Ponsonby.

A.S. Bobbie C.Reid. Betty Geordie Sarah Gaspard Ponsonby
Audrey Xandra.

SILVA PLANA.

Suvretta House, the hotel we stayed at in St Moritz, was run by an Englishman, Colonel Bond. It was rather like staying in a private house party.

Sarah   A.S.   Rachel   Audvey   Xandra.

RIGHT: *As can be seen from this photograph, fashion in ski resorts has changed dramatically over the years.*

RIGHT: *A shooting lunch on the moor at Drumlanrig with my father.*

BELOW RIGHT: *My mother with nurse Dickie who looked after my father during his last illness.*

skaters. We joined many friends and acquaintances at the Suvretta Hotel, at that time run by an Englishman, Colonel Bond, who appeared to be a tremendous friend of everybody. It was like staying in a private house party. Those one did not know already one soon became friendly with, through meeting over a 'sun downer' or joining up for dinner together.

There were no ski-lifts and it was quite an effort struggling up the slopes to the start of the runs. Luckily, as a result of much riding, I was very fit and had the necessary muscles for controlling my skis. It did not take me long to get going easily without too many tumbles. Sometimes amongst the breathless climbers one would find Lady Astor, with her sister Mrs Brand alongside. They were expert skiers and enjoyed the fun as much as anyone, in spite of being elderly compared to most of us. Nancy Astor, through her fame and force of character, tended to preside over the party. She was a lot of fun but could sometimes be rather cruel and sarcastic, as when she deliberately embarrassed people in public. During a lull at dinner, for instance, she might suddenly fasten on some shy young girl and shout across the table, 'Who is that young man I saw you having chocolate with?' The

victim, not surprisingly, was apt to be mortified by the unexpected attention which was focused on her.

Occasionally we would go skiing by moonlight. This entailed riding in a snow cat — a vehicle with caterpillar wheels — which took us to the start of a long run down a wide track through the forest. It was most romantic, with the full moon casting blue shadows from the snow-covered fir trees on either side. At the end of the run we assembled for hot soup at a chalet and then drove back to the hotel.

Sometimes we would go to Silsmaria, a small resort on the border with Italy. For this we hired a horse-drawn sleigh with three or four of us sitting inside and two following on skis holding on to a rope. With tinkling bells attached to the horses and beautiful scenery all around us, this was a charming experience.

We had friends practising for the Cresta Run and sometimes went to watch them. Xandra and I persuaded them to arrange for us to go down the last lap one Sunday morning when the Run was closed to competitions. I am sure this must have been most irresponsible on their part; however, as it snowed heavily the night before, the jaunt was not possible. Just as well, no doubt.

A.S.   ANGELA.   B.Q.   PHYLLIS

ANGELA

NURSE DICKIE.   M.B.Q.

The year of 1929 represented something of a watershed in my life. Apart from anything else it was then that my father first showed symptoms of the cancer — undiagnosed at the time — from which he was eventually to die. It was not an easy period. My mother was devoted to my father and terribly worried about his health, but her anxiety and fuss irritated him. Things were not improved by the arrival of a permanent nurse in the form of Miss Dickie. He enjoyed her company and showed his gratitude by giving her a pearl necklace and fur coat. Not unnaturally this made my mother jealous. I think she was also slightly jealous of me, because I too at that time was favoured by my father. As a result I felt uneasy at home and restless in other ways. That I had not fulfilled the promise I had made in return for my life nagged at my conscience. Boyfriends were getting over-friendly and increasingly I did not know how to cope. I began to realise that the people I met were 'birds of a feather' and that the young men, in particular, seemed to think of nothing but hunting, shooting, fishing and point-to-points. I felt the need to find a different kind of life, one where I would be able to meet other types of people.

It was at this time that my Uncle Francis Scott, his wife and two lovely little girls arrived at Drumlanrig on holiday from their farm in Kenya. They suggested I come and stay with them for an extended visit and assured me that there were plenty of things I could do to make myself useful. Coming at a moment of such uncertainty the offer could not have been more tempting, but nevertheless I found it hard to accept. There was my hunting to give up and the sadness of leaving my father. Uncle Francis and his family left. I remained in doubt. Then one day when I was out

Boyfriends were getting very friendly and increasingly I did not know how to cope. I wanted to find a different kind of life.

A.S.   COLIN.

for a walk, turning the question over in my mind for the umpteenth time, a roe deer suddenly started up. It leapt a fence and galloped away towards the hills. 'There,' I thought. 'That's an omen. I must get up and gallop away too.' And I went and wrote a letter of acceptance.

PART THREE

Kenya

*Kenya was so peaceful then. I photographed this
typical scene near Nakuru.*

Chapter Ten

DELORAINE

T WAS WITH SOME CONCERN AND SAD
ness that I made this great decision to move
so far away, leaving my father in none too
good a state of health. I knew he appreciated my company and was amused by my flow of
local gossip and any funny stories I could collect,
not to mention my help with the crossword
puzzles. He was horrfied at the idea of my going
to Kenya, which for him represented nothing but
Uncle Francis's farming debts. Nevertheless he
was very fond of his younger brother and worried
about his severely wounded leg; perhaps he
guessed that I could be of much help to him and
his wife and family. Whatever his feelings, he
generously gave me my ticket for the journey and
money for a car and petrol — and, much to my
relief, I later discovered he had also cleared my
large overdraft at the bank!

The days of the settlers who went to make a
life in Kenya in the early decades of the present
century are delightfully recalled in *They made it their
Home* – a collection of stories with an introduction by Elspeth Huxley, published in 1962. Of
all the books I have read about Kenya, this covers
the period before and while I was there best.

When my uncle and aunt first came, with their
two small children and the indomitable Miss

ELSPETH HUXLEY. PHYLLIS GRIGG. "BUDGY" O'HAGAN

*A party held for the Governor's conference, at
Government House, Nairobi.*

Loder, my aunt's maid, they had to live in three
mud huts while they organised the building of
the house, which was later to be named Deloraine
after a hill on the family estate in Selkirkshire.
Bricks were made locally by Indians, who were
the only people capable of that sort of work.
Deloraine was one of the few houses in the
colony to have a second storey. By the time I
arrived there was already a lovely garden of well-
kept lawns and shrubs.

Miss Loder had established herself as something of a local legend. She was everything:
housekeeper, nanny, cook, dairymaid. My aunt
left her in complete control and accordingly she
would be on the go all day — cursing, screaming,
shouting and generally bullying the African
'boys', who took it all with the greatest good
humour. There were many house-boys who were
completely uneducated and spoke only Swahili.
They could not have been more good humoured
or obliging. The same applied to the workers on
the farm. But in most cases the men were
incorrigibly lazy. They would sit gossiping, then
dash out and work madly at the sound of
someone coming and stop the moment the coast
was clear again. This was tradition. The women
worked, the men did not — to do so, for them,

Pam and Moy Scott between
the Sladen girls who lived
nearby. Pam still lives
at Deloraine.

GERALDINE SLADEN. PAM. MOY   RUTH SLADEN.

was an indignity. The attitude was general but its effects were particularly noticeable at Deloraine because of my uncle's tolerant spirit.

Francis Scott was one of those people who never thought ill of anyone. He had the most useless manager, but he never checked up on him or the men, and when it was brought to his attention he just dismissed it with a sigh and said 'Maybe, but you'll never get anyone better.' The fact is he was not very interested in farming and the farm suffered as a result: fences went unmended and crops uncollected. Maize was the main crop and there was a dairy herd, which provided milk for our tea and cream for our porridge.

Uncle Francis was not much helped by Aunt Eileen in running the farm. She adored him but Kenya was something she preferred to ignore. She loved music and the theatre and must have missed these sadly. While the other settlers' wives rolled their sleeves up and mucked in, Aunt Eileen carried on in the style to which she had been accustomed as a daughter of the Viceroy. She seemed to spend most of her time reading in bed, but when she got up she dressed impeccably, always wearing gloves, a hat and carrying a parasol. At Deloraine she

hung old family portraits on the walls and insisted on silver for every meal. There was nothing like it in the colony. However, she did design and start the lovely gardens that now have flowering shrubs of brilliant colours nine or ten feet tall and she also made a kitchen-garden on either side of a small stream, in which were grown many English vegetables, including asparagus. Fig trees did well but the figs had to be enclosed in little bags, as otherwise the monkeys ate them.

Mida, when visiting Deloraine in the early days, was invited to a dance some forty miles away and a young man offered to drive her there. On hearing this Aunt Eileen felt bound to accompany her as chaperone. A deck chair was erected in the back of the box-body car, and with Aunt Eileen perched on high, they set off. Mida and the young man chatted away and arrived at the party in no time, only to discover to their horror that Aunt Eileen had vanished. Everyone was in a state of confused indecision as to what should be done when, to their profound relief, she re-appeared in someone else's car. Her rescuers had been travelling through the bush when, to their amazement, they had found their way blocked by a lady sitting in a deck chair under an elegant parasol.

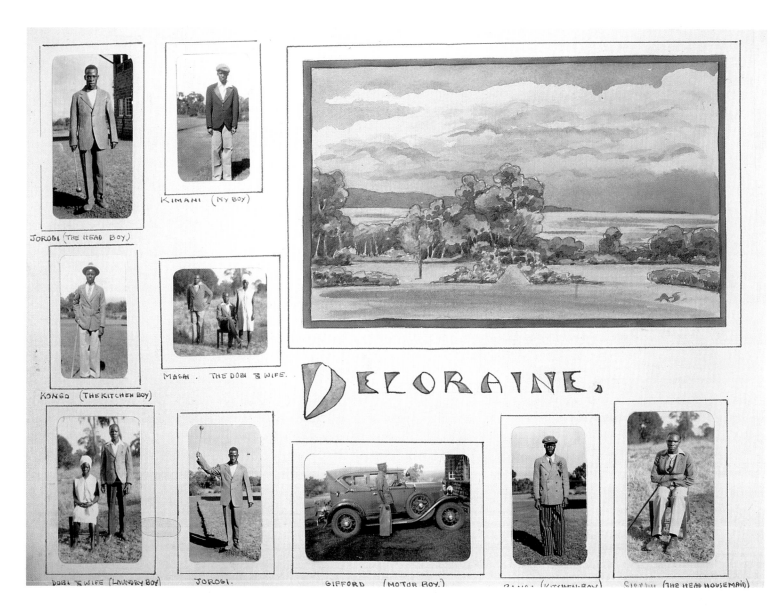

JOROGI (THE HEAD BOY.)

KIMANI (MY BOY)

KONGO (THE KITCHEN BOY)

MASAI. THE DOBI & WIFE.

DELORAINE.

DOBI & WIFE (LAUNDRY BOY)

JOROGI.

GIFFORD (MOTOR BOY.)

(KITCHEN BOY)

(THE HEAD HOUSEMAID)

The household at Deloraine. My boy, Kimani,
is at the top on the right.

THE FARM

Deloraine was named after a hill on the family estate in Selkirkshire

It was typical that when I first arrived in Africa she insisted on only two things: that I should wear a red flannel spine pad and a red lining to my hat. Everyone wore a wide-brimmed felt hat in those days as protection from what were generally considered to be the lethal rays of the sun. Both spine pad and hat proved tiresome in a hot country. I wore them religiously at first, but when I arrived on my second trip I found, to my relief, that such garments were no longer thought to be necessary.

Of course not all the African men were lazy. Uncle Francis was especially blessed in that he had a Masai tribesman of extraordinary devotion as his personal servant. This was unusual because the Masai were the proudest of tribes and normally deemed any kind of service beneath contempt; but Ehru, my uncle's servant, was exceptional in that a white man had saved his life.

Uncle Francis and Aunt Eileen on a visit home. In Kenya Eileen carried on in the style to which she was accustomed as a Viceroy's daughter.

During the First World War he had been a soldier in the Kenya African rifles and, after a skirmish with the Germans, had been wounded and left to die on the battlefield. One of the settlers, Mervyn Ridley, his officer at the time, bravely rescued him and subsequently saw to it that he was nursed back to health. Ehru, in return, pledged his life to him. Mervyn Ridley was in no need of further employees at that point, so he passed him on to my uncle, in whose service he proved the most faithful servant anyone could ever want and was dearly loved by the whole household.

I was scarcely less privileged in my own servant, Kimani. He was in his mid-twenties and acted as my maid, motor boy and bodyguard, in fact as everything. Kimani was assigned to me as soon as I arrived. I paid him sixpence a day, which covered his food and all living expenses, and I

THE RETURN OF THE BOXBODY HUDSON !

Boxbody cars were most usual in Kenya in those
days — mine was a Citroen. Roads, even the
main roads out of Nairobi, were tracks of mud.
After rain the soil, known as 'black cotton',
became impassable, like a peat bog.

NDARE NGARE

THE LORD HIGH HAM CUTTER

EHRU   LAZARO

IMPISHI.   GREATER BUSTARD.   A.S.

On safari in Kenya. In those days there were no tourists at all, even in areas as famous as the Masai Mara.

NDARE NGARE.

JIMMIE

THE NORTHERN FRONTIER.

? !!

NDARE NGARE.

*Ndare Ngare on the Northern Frontier was full
of every kind of wildlife.*

At that time Uganda seemed such a happy country, with a friendly smile on every well-fed face. Alas, the same cannot be said today.

AS. BUYING ORANGES AT KAMPALA.

bought him his clothes – several pairs of shorts, some loose, white, shirt-like garments and a red tarboosh and blankets. If needed, I would also buy some extras for him, like wood. We motored hundreds of miles alone together with no trace of anxiety on my part. No one could have been a more dependable or trustworthy companion. If we stayed somewhere and he suspected another boy of mischief, he would ask me to hand over my money, jewellery and anything else I had that might tempt a thief and would take it all into his own safe-keeping for the night. To have such confidence nowadays would be rare.

Once Kimani came to me and asked if he could have the following day off. I agreed but asked him the reason. 'I have to cook something that I must take to a particular old tree because my little son is ill and the witch-doctor says I must do that to make him well again,' he said. 'But Kimani,' I remonstrated, 'I thought you were a Christian?' 'Oh yes I am,' he said seriously, 'but it's just as well to be on the safe side.' This conversation was, of course, conducted in Swahili. Few Africans at that time spoke English.

On one occasion his zeal for my well-being was overdone. Finding some brand-new laces in my shoes instead of the old worn-out and knotted ones, I asked him where he had got them. With great pride he said he had taken them out of one of the other Bwana's shoes.

'But that's awful, Kimani,' I said in horror. 'It's stealing!'

'Oh no,' he replied confidently. 'Kimani not stealing for Kimani, it is for Memsahib.'

'But that's worse,' I said, 'Because it makes me a thief.'

'Oh no,' said Kimani. 'Memsahib did not do it.'

There was nothing more to be said.

Necessity soon forced me to pick up enough of the language to make myself understood. Every white person was given a name by the Africans. My aunt, for instance, always wore earrings so she was called Memsahib 'Kingeli', which means earrings. When I arrived for the first time I was named Memsahib 'Mhowa', which means flower, because I liked to pick bunches of wild flowers for my room. Giggling hordes of children from the village would invariably follow me around on my walks, mimicking my movements with glee and picking vast bunches themselves which they would subsequently press on me. They just thought I was rather dotty to do such a thing, but the local witch-doctor was positively disapproving. If I passed his house on my way home he would give me a nasty look which I returned with my sweetest smile, annoying him even more. My Memsahib 'Mhowa' days, however, were relatively short-lived because, when it was learned that I had flown away and returned again by aeroplane, I was rechristened Memsahib 'Ndegi' meaning bird. There were only a few private planes in Kenya at the time and people, in consequence, who travelled in them were viewed with understandable awe by the locals.

Kenya was so peaceful then. The Africans one met were always smiling and contented; there were spectacular amounts of game of every species and the bush, as one drove along, was a glory of

magnificent cedars, podocarpus and crimson flame trees. In other ways, however, travelling was not always a joy. The roads, even the main roads out of Nairobi, were formed only of packed mud, which soon deteriorated into wheel tracks, often rutted so deeply that you had to move to one side or the other and make a fresh track. Much of the soil, which was known as 'black cotton', became impassable and like a peat bog after rain.

Box-body cars — mine was a Citroen — were the most commonly used and one had to put chains on the tyres when it was wet. A roll of chicken-wire was also carried to lay on the mud or on a sandy river bed if the chains could still not get a grip. Bridges were a rarity, and when in place usually consisted of no more than a couple of stout planks to which the wheels had to be precariously aligned. Often fords or dry river-beds suddenly became torrents after electric storms had broken out in a different part of the country, upstream from where one was. At these times the motor boy, who was always in attendance, would survey the prospects and, if necessary, lead the car through the flood, with water up to his knees. If it proved too deep, there was nothing to be done but wait till the level dropped. As a result, bedding and food were usually carried. The chances of meeting other travellers were remote.

When the Prince of Wales visited Kenya, my aunt and uncle, my friend Marye Pole Carew and I were all invited to join the house party for him at Government House in Nairobi. The Prince was staying a few days before going on safari. He objected strongly to the rule that he should always be accompanied by a doctor, and this caused some worry amongst those responsible for the expedition. In the end, unknown to him, Dr Bainbridge, an eminent Nairobi doctor, was sent along disguised as the driver of the royal car.

It was not long, sadly, before Marye had to leave as she was expected back in England shortly. I wanted to go to Zanzibar and so did she, so we decided to combine a trip to the Sultanate with her homeward voyage. It did not sound too difficult to arrange. 'You can always get a ship from Mombasa to Zanzibar and back,' somebody said. 'You just go to the booking office in Mombasa.' We went, and were told, on the contrary, that the only ship due to sail for Zanzibar in the immediate future was a Japanese cargo boat. 'Is that all right?' we asked anxiously. 'Oh yes', they assured us. It only took six passengers,

S.S. "CANADA MARU"

Commander, K. Taniguchi.

Friday 30th May. 1930.

DINNER
****
(SOUP)
Consomme a la Gauloise.
(FISH)
Boiled Fish, Anchovy sauce.
(ENTREE)
Macaroni Tin-bell Tomato sauce.
Pork Chop with Jardienire.
Curry and Rice.
(JOINT)
Boiled Corned Beef & Cabbage.
Roast Mutton Brown au Jus.
(VEGETABLES)
Potatoes Boiled. Browned.
Leeks au Jus.
(SWEET)
Custard Pudding.
(DESSERT)
Fruit in Season.
Assorted Nuts.
Cheese.
Tea or Coffee.

ARAB DHOW

When my friend, Mary Carew Pole, had to
return to England, I accompanied her as far as
Zanzibar. We travelled on a Japanese cargo
boat. The crew were very polite but giggled
at everything we said.

but it was clean and comfortable. You embarked at 5 p.m. and arrived in Zanzibar by 9 the following morning.

Once on board we were rather surprised to find that the dining-room was shared with the crew, and consisted of a long room in the middle of the ship with a huge table down the middle and three passengers' cabins giving on to it from along each side. The crew were very polite but giggled uncontrollably at everything we said, and with each lurch of the ship throughout the night our cabin doors embarrassingly swung open to reveal us to anyone who might still be sitting at the table.

In Zanzibar we stayed with a Mr Battiscombe and attended a dinner and dance for the Sultan's birthday. The Sultan was a charming old man, and very pleased to see us because it gave him a chance to return the hospitality he had received from my family on his trips to England. He had even been up to the Borders, where he had been given a grand tour by Walter including an inspection of the Buccleuch's pack of fox-hounds in the hunt kennels at St Boswell's. It was both odd and comforting to speak of such homely things in such an exotic place. The next day he most courteously accompanied us on a tour of the island and I made a pilgrimage of my own to see a memorial plaque in honour of my uncle, Dick Bridgeman, who had died there while on duty with the navy in the First World War. He had been in an engagement with the German battleship *Koenigsberg*, which had taken refuge in a Tanganyikan river.

The Sultan of Zanzibar had stayed with us in the Borders and was delighted to return our hospitality. The Residency Ball marked George V's birthday.

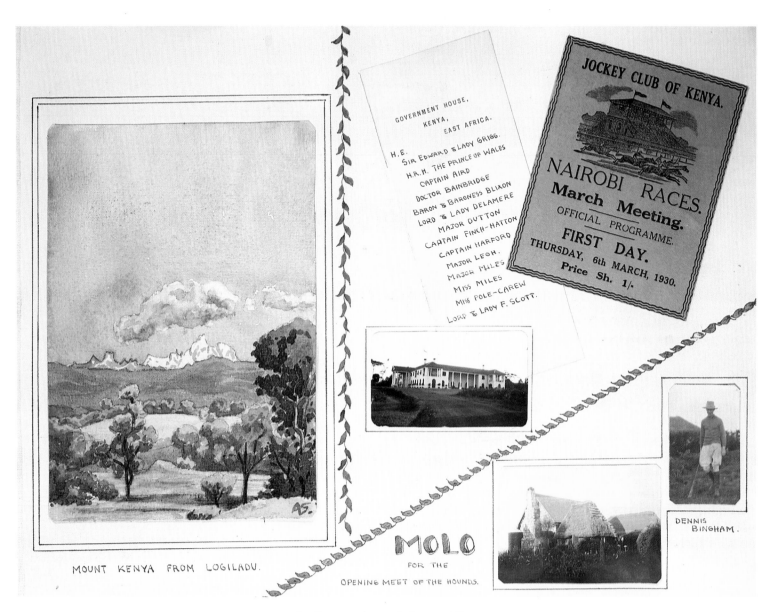

MOUNT KENYA FROM LOGILADU.

GOVERNMENT HOUSE,
KENYA,
EAST AFRICA.

H.E.
SIR EDWARD & LADY GRIGG.
H.R.H. THE PRINCE OF WALES
CAPTAIN AIRD
DOCTOR BAINBRIDGE
BARON & BARONESS BLIXON
LORD & LADY DELAMERE
MAJOR DUTTON
CAPTAIN FINCH-HATTON
CAPTAIN HARFORD
MAJOR LEGH.
MAJOR MILES
MISS MILES
MISS POLE-CAREW
LORD & LADY F. SCOTT.

JOCKEY CLUB OF KENYA.

NAIROBI RACES.
March Meeting.
OFFICIAL PROGRAMME.
FIRST DAY.
THURSDAY, 6th MARCH, 1930.
Price Sh. 1/-

MOLO
FOR THE
OPENING MEET OF THE HOUNDS.

DENNIS
BINGHAM.

*An album page showing the diversity of Kenyan
life. I helped build the Bingham's house at Molo
which appears in the bottom right-hand corner.*

Chapter Eleven

SETTLERS
AND SAFARIS

I STAYED IN KENYA FOR OVER A YEAR ON THAT FIRST VISIT It was a wonderful period of freedom for me. I revelled in the fact that I could dress informally most of the time, in trousers, boots and cotton check shirts, and be at the farm one minute and off in my car on some adventure the next. I suppose I was a kind of pre-beatnik, but I also thrived on the responsibility; responsibility not just for myself but also, to an important extent, for my uncle and aunt. Aunt Eileen went to England as often as she could, so I was left to look after Uncle Francis and, since he was frequently away in Nairobi on government business, I was often the ultimate authority in the day-to-day running of the farm.

The climate was perfect at Deloraine because it was 8,000 feet above sea level and life there was very informal and the greatest fun. Polo at Njoro, some fifteen miles away, was a popular excuse for people to foregather on a Sunday, and teams would arrive from quite a distance away. Uncle Francis was a keen player and, in spite of the 'gammy' leg from his time as a soldier, a very good one. I made many friends and accepted mounts for hunting and gymkhanas. The atmosphere was delightfully happy-go-lucky. A man who lived about twenty-five miles from the polo ground would unharness his ponies after a match, give them a smack and trust them to find their own way home.

There were also three packs of hounds in those days and we hunted a little buck called a dick-dick, which lived in a particular kind of scrubby terrain. I never saw a snake during my whole time in Kenya and the greatest hazard when riding was being tripped by a hidden pig hole. Thankfully most of the horses seemed to have a sixth sense about this – often they were polo ponies – and accidents rarely occurred.

That summer I went to a very different part of Kenya to stay for a few weeks in a 'banda' (or native hut) just south of Mombasa. It was refreshing to be at the seaside. No one had swimming-pools in those days and all water was treated with the greatest caution for fear it harboured the often deadly bilharzia worm. There were few people on the coast and the only buildings were the three or four open-sided bandas. The most famous inhabitant was a one hundred-year-old tortoise. Everyone going to Mombasa would be photographed sitting on its back. I read some years later that it did not die of old age but had the misfortune to be flattened by a lorry in whose shade it had been taking a siesta.

Later that year, after I had made a wonderful safari with Uncle Francis to visit a coffee plantation he had a share in on the borders of Tanganyika and Nyasaland, I helped with the first visit by a group of English schoolboys to the colony. The party, about twelve in number, were put up by various families round about. At Deloraine we had the master in charge, who happened to be the son of the Dean of Windsor, and two of his pupils. When writing his name in the visitors' book at the end of his stay the master rather pompously wrote Windsor Castle as his address. Much to his subsequent annoyance, the boys, who quite rightly considered him something of a snob, added the letters 'SS' in front of it.

The original English settlers, like Lord Delamere and Mervyn Ridley, initially came to hunt, it is true; but they stayed to farm and so did their successors. They treasured the animals and grew to be very anti-shooting. They might go out with a gun to protect their crops or livestock or to get something for the pot or the dogs, but they heartily

RIGHT: On the steps with 'Boy' and Genessie Long at their home, Nderit.

BELOW: 'Boy' and Lord Furness viewing flamingoes on Lake Nakuru.

BOY LONG.   GLADY DELAMERE.   GENESSY LONG.   A.S.

despised the trophy shooting of the big-game hunters.

Kenya may have been regarded as a den of iniquity, but the settlers on the whole were good and worthy people. It was just the few who used it as a bolt-hole to escape their creditors back in England that gave it a bad name. The most extensive landowner was Lord Delamere, renowned for his unique distinction of being a blood-brother of the Masai. Another legendary figure was Ewart Grogan, who had walked from Cairo to the Cape in order to persuade the girl he loved to marry him — which she did! Both these formidable characters took a leading part in the political life and welfare of the country.

Much gossip surrounded the settlers of Happy Valley and this has only increased with time, but most of them were respectable and serious farmers. If there was a glamorous couple,

it was undoubtedly 'Boy' and Genessie Long, who set off their good looks with beautifully cut and chosen clothes. 'Boy' invariably sported riding-boots and a very dashing sombrero trimmed with snakeskin. They had a magnificent estate overlooking Lake Nakura, now an attractive game park.

Here I met Evelyn Waugh, who had just arrived from the coronation of Haile Selassie where Prince Henry had been representing King George V. Although only in Kenya for a few days, Waugh had already succeeded in making himself very unpopular. He seemed to take a malicious pleasure in irritating people. One evening we had a picnic dinner. When the moon came out he put on a very conspicuous hat and announced, 'I'm told the Kenya moon is dangerous and makes people decidedly odd. I think I'd better keep my hat on.' During our stay the

*From left to right; Donald Handeman,
John Ramsden, 'Dina Handeman,
myself and Bobby Roberts.*

DONALD. JOHN. 'DINA. A.S. BOBBY ROBERTS

Longs and their near-neighbours suffered a great deal of damage from a huge grass fire. From the house we watched this inferno rage in the darkness. Although a beautiful and awe-inspiring sight, to many of the party it represented the loss of their most precious pasture, so its beauty was not for them a matter of the first concern. But Evelyn Waugh would not stop. 'Oh, what a wonderful sight!' he kept exclaiming. 'Isn't it magnificent?'

A character who was undeniably responsible for giving Kenya some of its reputation was Raymond de Trafford — a remarkable individual who was known to most people as 'the Borstal Boy'. He had suffered the indignity of being shot by his wife. Before I left for Africa everybody said, 'Beware of the Borstal Boy. Be sure to lock your door if he's around!' I never thought any more about this till one night, when staying with friends, a car drove up unexpectedly and in he walked. Having been waylaid by a sudden deluge, he was looking for some dinner and a bed for the night.

The visitors' bedrooms were in a guest-house across the garden from the main building, as is normally the case in Kenya, and my hostess, while finding herself obliged to put Raymond up, clearly felt

somewhat uneasy on my behalf. I guessed that she had warned him to behave like a gentleman. When bedtime arrived the two of us crossed the garden to our little guest-house. Sure enough, after a pause he called to me from his side of the hut, 'It's awfully cold, isn't it!' I called back, 'I've got a rug in my car. Would you like it?' 'No thanks,' came the disappointed reply. I was slightly unnerved by this so I crept to the door and tried to turn the key without him hearing, but it would not turn. 'It's no use trying to lock your door,' he said, 'because I know it doesn't work. Would you like me to come and push the chest-of-drawers up against it?'

Over the following years I got to know Raymond reasonably well and found he had a good side to him and was a well-read and amusing companion. He was one of those people who could not bring himself to stop gambling, but he was not in the least embarrassed at the resulting failure to pay his debts.

The great hostess was Idina Erroll, wife of Joss Erroll, who was later the victim of the infamous murder. She was very nice to meet; it was just that she did seem to have had rather a lot of husbands. One evening when I was at her house I came into the drawing-room to be

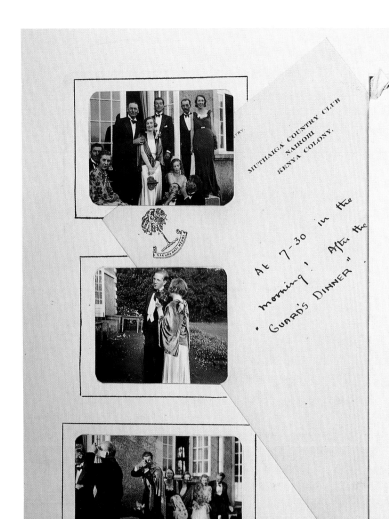

MUTHAIGA COUNTRY CLUB
NAIROBI
KENYA COLONY.

At 7-30 in the
morning! After the
"Gunid's Dinner".

Kenya Polo Association.

PROGRAMME

OF

POLO TOURNAMENT

TO BE HELD ON THE

NAIROBI POLO CLUB GROUND.

CONNAUGHT OPEN CHAMPIONSHIP CUP

31st December, 1931, and 3rd January, 1932.

JUNIOR MCMILLAN (LIMITED HANDICAP) CUP

31st December, 1931, and 2nd and 3rd January, 1932.

SOMALI CUP.

ORDER OF PLAY.

Thurs. 31st Dec.	CONNAUGHT CUP 3.00 p.m.	(a) NAIROBI v. NJORO.
	JR. MCMILLAN CUP 4.00 p.m.	(1) POLICE v. NJORO.
Fri. 1st Jan.	JR. MCMILLAN CUP 10.00 a.m.	(2) NAIROBI v. SERGOIT.
Sat. 2nd Jan.	JR. MCMILLAN CUP 10 a.m.	(3) Winners of (1) v. Rongai (bye) alternate chukkers with (4) Winners of (2) v. Mau-Molo (bye)
Sun. 3rd Jan.	CONNAUGHT CUP 3.30 p.m. FINAL.	Winners of (a) v. Muthaiga (bye)
	JR. MCMILLAN CUP 4.15 p.m. FINAL.	Winners of (3) v. Winners of (4)

A rare visit to Nairobi. On this occasion a polo
match must have been followed by the inevitable
party at the Muthaiga Club.

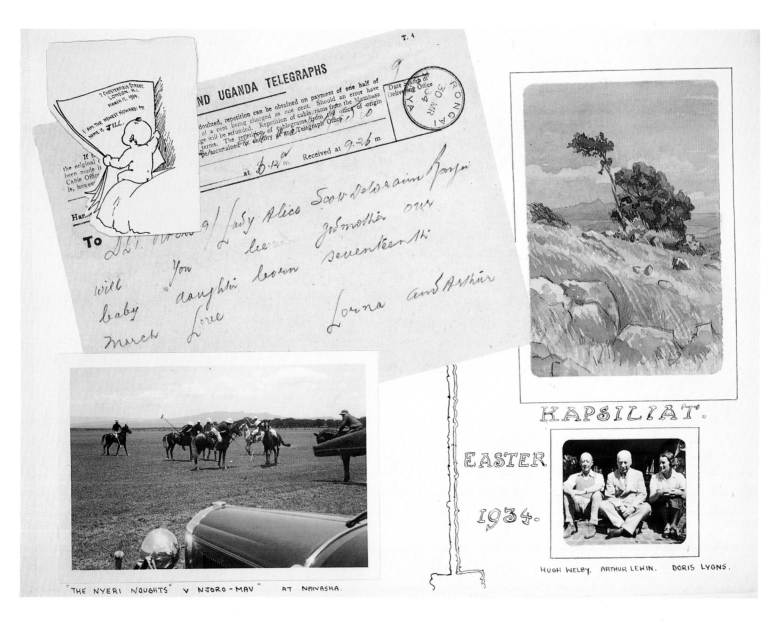

KAPSILIAT.

EASTER 1934.

HUGH WELBY. ARTHUR LEWIN. DORIS LYONS.

"THE NYERI NOUGHTS" V "NJORO-MAU" AT NAIVASHA.

Easter at Kapsiliat with Sybil and Mervyn Ridley.
Mervyn Ridley was one of the earliest settlers
in Kenya. The telegram was asking me to
be Godmother of Lorna and Arthur Howard's child.

told, 'Don't sit there or you'll be in the line of fire.' This was when Raymond de Trafford was threatening to shoot somebody. I think a lot of the trouble was that at those heights a little drink goes a long way. I am sure they got up to all sorts of mischief but if you were not interested they did not bother you. I'm not sure how much fun it was for Idina's child, the future Lady Erroll. I found her one morning wandering in the garden all by herself. She seemed to me to be a rather sad little thing.

It was the custom in Kenya to be out of bed by about 6 a.m. so as to make the most of the day before the heat set in. At Deloraine I would often follow the game tracks up into the forest behind the farm, and thanks to this I soon made friends with one of the Kenyan forest tribes, the Wandarobo. One of this tribe, Arap Lesse, befriended me and acted as my guide. He showed me buffalo and other animals I would never have seen otherwise, and even promised to take me to see the rarest of woodland antelopes, an animal called the bongo. Teddy Brook had always wanted to shoot a bongo, so I wrote and told him to come along. He was delighted at the idea and hurriedly made plans to get the necessary shooting permit. News of this greatly upset the head

game-warden, who hated people to go out on this kind of expedition unless he was along to help.

When the day arrived we set off on foot with Marslie Truman (a near neighbour) as chaperone and a dozen or more Africans to carry our camping equipment. Arap Lesse led us into the depths of the forest, where we pitched camp by a spring in an open glade. Early next morning we left Marslie to spend a peaceful day with her knitting and a rifle in case buffalo should appear, and started to climb five or six hundred feet through thick forest to the high and remote area frequented by the bongo. The camp itself was above 8,000 feet so the thinness of the air made the climb tiring, in addition to which we needed to keep very quiet and not to tread heavily on the mass of dry twigs that littered our path.

At last we spied the bongo grazing amongst some bamboo. Teddy fired and down she went. We both felt triumphant but also sad to see the death of such a rare and beautiful creature. Arap Lesse skinned the beast there and then; Teddy got his head and I the covers for two large photograph albums which I still have. Having secured his bongo Teddy returned home. In 1933, during my second stay, he and Prince

LEFT: *At Deloraine, preparing to leave on safari.*

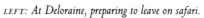

ABOVE: *On safari. In the back row, from left to right, are Uncle Francis, myself, Mervyn Ridley and Aunt Eileen: in the front row are Gifford, Ehru, Nhora and Kikelli.*

FROM OUR CAMP AT NGARE NDARE.

I started painting in Kenya to record the colours
which was not then possible with photography.

THE RIFT VALLEY & ABERDARE Mᵗˢ FROM THE BINGHAM'S FARM.

 Short of money on my return to London,
I exhibited my watercolours in a Bond Street
gallery, selling 190 guineas worth!

My original title for this photograph, taken near Deloraine, was 'The Wanderoboo wife at home'.

Henry went big-game hunting in the Sudan, but they did not come on to Kenya. Prince Henry was never to visit the colony while I was there.

I returned to England in the early spring. It was the best possible moment to arrive back home. Friends and relations seemed glad to see me and hear about 'darkest' Africa, as it was looked upon by many of them. I must have changed quite a bit, having gained self-confidence from the experience and a greater knowledge of people and their ways of living and thinking. I lost no time in going to visit my sisters and special friends but I saw little of Prince Henry; he was busy soldiering at Tidworth and at the end of the summer got shingles. I saw him briefly again while I was staying with Walter and his family at Eildon – he was with his brother Prince George, the Duke of Kent. They had friends in Kenya and were interested to have news of them.

By now I felt more than ready to return to the carefree existence of Africa. This time I stocked up with painting materials, having found great satisfaction experimenting with watercolours; and Teddy had lent me a cine-camera, a novelty at that time.

Back at Deloraine my friends the Binghams looked in one day with news that gold had been discovered near Kakamega, a district just north of Lake Victoria. They asked if I would like to join them and a friend of theirs who had 'pegged' a claim. Always ready for a new adventure, I accepted on the spot. Finding the place proved more difficult than we had expected. When we asked locals the way, they just roared with laughter and said, 'Ah! Musungo ku-chimba', which is Swahili for 'White man digging', evidently something they found amusing!

We eventually found a camp by the riverside, where we settled in amongst our fellow prospectors, one of whom turned out to be Raymond de Trafford. Before staking a claim one had to pay a token fee for a piece of paper from the District Commissioner's office, on which were entered name, address and claim number. Then all one had to do was to nail the paper to a post, stick it in the centre of the designated piece of ground and hope for the best. A friendly South African showed us how to toss the earth and gravel in a basin of water, chucking out the contents at intervals so that the pieces of gold, being heavier than the rest, would remain behind till the final shake. I found one small nugget.

While the Binghams went to Kisumo, a few hours' journey further

RIGHT: *PLEASE TRY SHOUTING*
BEFORE SHOOTING. On this occasion
there was no need for either.

FAR RIGHT: *The hunt for gold at Kakamega.*

on, to try to obtain an order for the cream and cheese they made on their farm, I and the South African went to investigate a claim belonging to a neighbour who had had to go away on farm business. It was in a small stream off the main river, and we struggled along on hands and knees as the undergrowth was thick and came down to a foot or so above the water. I went in front so as to avoid getting branches flicked back into my face and, on rounding the final bend, came face to face with three astonished and rather angry-looking men. 'What do you want?' one of them asked darkly. I explained that the claim belonged to a friend of mine. 'No longer,' replied another of the men, with a nasty laugh. 'Our claim is pegged here now.' So that was that — there was obviously no point in arguing. I paid another visit there two years later and found a small town had sprung up. In the evening we went to dance at 'The Eldorado', a noisy saloon where the prospectors gathered. It was all like a 'Wild West' film.

Being so happy in Kenya, I stayed till the middle of 1931 before finally dragging myself back to England. Disapproving of my visits to Kenya, my father warned me that if I was determined to go again it

*The natural beauty of Kenya is something I have
never forgotten.*

A view of Mount Kenya.

"MAC"   A.S.

would have to be at my own expense. This confronted me for the first time with the task of earning money, and I decided to hold an exhibition of my watercolours.

Painting was not something that I had done much of before I went to Kenya, but when I got there I found myself taking it up simply because (this being before the days of colour photography) there was no other way of recording the colouring of the place. My painting expeditions proved to be one of the most rewarding features of my Kenyan life — peaceful, instructive and full of incident.

Monkeys were particularly mischievous. Once I left my painting for a short time to take a stroll and returned to find one holding my brushes. He ran off chattering excitedly and climbed a tree — and that was the last I saw of them. Monkeys were at their worst and most excitable if one was with a dog, and it was not unknown for them to jump down in a gang on such occasions, if they saw the dog unattended, and to attack and sometimes even kill it.

Another time I came face to face with a leopard. It was eating a buck it had just killed and looked at me with great surprise. I was not quite sure what to do, but decided to walk backwards, staring hard at it and whistling 'The Road to the Isles'. This display of sang-froid succeeded and the leopard galloped away. Leopards too were known to go for dogs — it was even said that they would take one from inside a house, given the opportunity — but none of the animals had a reputation for attacking humans and it was never thought the slightest bit dangerous for me to go out alone.

I succeeded in fixing myself up with an exhibition of these Kenyan watercolours at

PETER   JIMMIE   A.S.   FRANCIS

Walker's Galleries in New Bond Street. I am sure the show met with much more kindly reviews than would be the case today. Even *The Times* gave me several column inches, including the compliment that: 'In Africa the artist seems to have risen to the occasion and, with imagination stimulated by unusual shapes and colours, produced a series of records which are interesting pictorially as well as from the topographical point of view.' I exhibited sixty-four pictures and sold 190 guineas-worth of them at an average of about five guineas apiece.

This was a great help to my finances. Only weeks before the exhibition I had had to travel by overnight bus from London for a party in Dumfriesshire, simply because I could not afford the train. As it was my first time on such a coach, I was rather disconcerted when we stopped at intervals through the night. 'I don't think I'll bother to come out, thank you,' I told my neighbours, in answer to their anxious invitations. 'Oh, but you must!' they replied, looking at me in horror. I thought, Oh dear — something awful must happen if one doesn't get

A picnic in the grass by Mount Kenya. Despite what one would expect I never saw a snake during my whole time in Kenya.

out, so out I got and joined them for large meals washed down with tea in the all-night cafés.

Aunt Eileen had returned to England to look after her mother and to be near her children, who were now at boarding-school; and Uncle Francis had finally decided to have his bad leg amputated. His need for help and companionship gave me a good excuse to go out to Kenya for a third time. The money from the watercolour exhibition enabled me to pay for my passage and Billy gave me a further £30 with which to buy a tent, the ones at Deloraine all being very old and dilapidated. I went to Teddy Brook for his expert advice.

'Where can I get a nice tent for £30?' I asked.
'Leave it to me,' he said, and in due course a lovely tent arrived with a bill for £30. The first time I used this tent in Kenya it caused a great sensation.

'What a marvellous tent!' some authority exclaimed. 'I wish I could get one.'

 *From the main road between Nakuru
and Naivasha.*

A view of Jaipur. My family persuaded me to visit George in India, where he was stationed with the 10th Royal Hussars.

'Why don't you?' I asked.

'Far too expensive,' he replied.

'Not at all,' I said with some satisfaction, 'it only costs £30.'

He laughed: 'Good Heavens — more like £300!'

And then I realised Teddy had asked the shop to send me a bill made out for £30 and paid the rest himself.

When my uncle was attending the Legislative Council in Nairobi, I was now left at Deloraine more or less in charge, aided, fortunately, by 'Loder', who stayed on as housekeeper. One of my worst moments came when it suddenly grew very dark at midday and, looking out, I saw clouds of smoke and a grass fire rapidly approaching from a mile or so away. Remembering instructions, I rang a bell to assemble the Africans. I told them to battle as best they could with the flames, while I dashed around opening gates and doors so that the animals could get out if need be. Luckily, the wind changed and the fire turned before reaching the garden.

My knowledge of first aid, learned while a Girl Guide and VAD came in most useful. One morning the gardener arrived carrying his big toe, which he had chopped off with a spade while making a bad shot at a clump of weeds. I shoved it on again and took him off with all speed to Nakuru Hospital where they fixed him up. He appeared quite unconcerned and obviously suffered little pain. Another time the 'Head Boy' (butler) arrived with bleeding fingers, having been bitten by a rat. The neat little criss-cross bandages I applied to each finger gave him immense satisfaction. He considered them extremely smart and decorative. When told they were no longer needed, he went off looking disappointed. He returned before long bringing a tearful child with bleeding fingers, obviously having suffered cuts from scissors or a knife. 'My son also bitten by rats and needs smart bandages,' he said hopefully. Needless to say I was much upset, and cross with him, but still had to do the best I could to bind up the small fingers.

Later that year I was persuaded by my family to go to India to visit my youngest brother George, who had recently joined the Tenth Royal Hussars at Lucknow. I found India a sad country compared to Kenya. You never saw a smile and the children seemed especially miserable and poverty-stricken, their eyes covered with flies. I was there at an awkward time, when Indians were beginning to agitate for

LEFT: At Camp Mar in Jaipur with George. We had all gathered there for a polo tournament; hence the marquee.

FAR LEFT: On the Kabul river, south of the Khyber Pass. The coat is an attempt at disguise.

independence and apt to be rude to English people. If you queued for a ticket or in a post office, the Indian ahead was inclined to go on with his business as long as possible, just so as to be annoying. They had recently for the first time been allowed to share railway carriages with Europeans and, when seeing one in a train, they would crowd in so as to demonstrate their new equality, even though compartments to either side stood empty. It was all rather trying, particularly when they chewed and spat out betel nut.

During this visit I had one great adventure, when I made a brief and illegal excursion into Afghanistan. Some Australians and their army friends offered to take me along if I was game for it. This sounded exciting so we arranged to set off the following morning. When my hostess heard of the plan, she said she would like to join the party but on no account must her husband know of it.

The two of us duly donned woolly Afghan overcoats and caps — with only our noses showing — hoping no one would stop us, for women were not allowed to enter the district. We got in by some secret overland route, only joining up with the main road once we were inside 'forbidden territory'. We then lunched with the army friends of the Australians and looked over the boundary gate from Afghanistan, before undergoing a rather frightening drive back down the Kabul Pass, a road of terrifying corners which was bordered by sheer drops and followed the winding course of the Kabul River far below. Eventually we emerged by the same secret track as we had come in, safe and undetected. News of the escapade later got about and there was a great row. I had left by then, but I had already realised what a frightfully stupid thing it was to have done.

Not long after, bad news of my father's health arrived and I was summoned home. It was the spring of 1935, and I set out on Jubilee Day. When we landed at Jubah we got off and listened to the King's speech on a very bad wireless in the District Commissioner's office. A fellow countryman had come over fifty miles out of the bush to listen — so there we sat, ears strained, only just able to hear the far-off voice.

PART FOUR

Marriage

It is with great pleasure that the King and Queen announce the betrothal of their dearly beloved son, the Duke of Gloucester, to the Lady Alice Montagu-Douglas-Scott, daughter of the Duke and Duchess of Buccleuch and Queensberry, to which union the King has gladly given his consent.

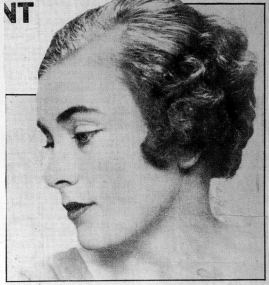

Lady Alice Montagu-Douglas-Scott. She is the third daughter of the Duke of Buccleuch.

ROYAL LOVERS AT SHOOTING PARTY

LADY ALICE, who is a well-known figure in social circles in the West End, is at present staying at Drumlanrig Castle, one of her father's seats, in Dumfries-shire, Scotland. The Duke and Duchess of Buccleuch are at Bowhill, Selkirk, another seat.

Drumlanrig Castle last night became the romantic domain of the fairy-books.

For in it was the traditional "Fair Lady of High Estate" who is destined to become the bride of one of the King's sons.

Lady Alice, together with the younger members of her family, had been shooting on the moors all day and returned to the centuries-old castle only a few hours before the news reached London from Balmoral Castle of her engagement.

At this time, however, it was still Lady Alice's secret from other members of the house party.

Romance Behind Shooting Party

An old retainer of the Buccleuch estate told the *Daily Mirror* of the surprise and joy the first news of the engagement caused.

"Lady Alice has been at Drumlanrig since the first few days of August," he said.

"The Duke of Gloucester visited the castle for three or four days about a fortnight ago, and with the other young people went shooting on the moors. The whole party were out together each day—they always go whether the weather be wet or fine. To all intents and purposes, it was just an ordinary party. No fuss was made of the Duke's visit.

"But I am sure that no one suspected the romance which lay behind his visit.

"You ask if Lady Alice knew that the announcement of her engagement was being made to-night. Well—(this with a laugh)—I am not so sure about that. I know her ladyship was expecting it to be made some time at the week-end.

"But, as a matter of fact, the romance has never been mentioned at Drumlanrig.

"Now that the engagement has been announced, there will be great rejoicing for miles around.

"Drumlanrig Castle is a wonderful setting for the occasion."

"Shoots" with the Camera

Artist and big-game hunter who "shoots" with the camera, Lady Alice Montagu-Douglas-Scott, has lived a vivid life.

She has spent a great deal of her time in Kenya, where her uncle, Lord Francis Scott, farms extensively. Her keen interest in big game hunting lies in "shooting" with the camera and in making records of the chase with the brush.

The press, as always, revelled in a Royal romance.

Chapter Twelve

MARRIAGE

I HAD AN INSTINCT THAT ONE DAY I WOULD MARRY PRINCE Henry and perhaps, without admitting it to myself, I had gone to Kenya for a last taste of freedom before abandoning a truly private life for ever. Almost as soon as I arrived back in England I went to stay with the Athlones for Ascot. Princess Alice probably knew Prince Henry was hoping to marry me and wished it herself, being very fond of us both. So I met him there and three months later we had announced our engagement.

It became fairly obvious what his intentions were. He did not shower me with flowers because he did not do things that way — but every time I saw him I realised more clearly what he wanted. He was terribly shy, though, and I am afraid I made it no easier for him by pretending not to notice. I was busy meeting friends and organising my second art exhibition of watercolours at the Walker Galleries — which incidentally proved even more successful than my début. But after a while we got in the habit of going for walks together in Richmond Park, which he liked for its privacy and as a place to exercise his dogs. Then one day at breakfast-time the telephone rang at 2 Grosvenor Place. Luckily my brother answered. It was the Press. 'What's this we hear about Lady Alice and Prince Henry?' they asked. 'First I've heard of it,' said Billy, pretending to be the footman, and this shook them off for a while.

Towards the end of the summer Prince Henry was posted to Catterick with his regiment, and I soon joined him in the north for a weekend party given by our old friend Teddy Brook for the opening of the grouse season. It was then that we got engaged. There was no formal declaration on his part — I think he just muttered an aside during one of our walks — nor was there any doubt of my acceptance. I was thirty-four, so I had had a very good innings. Apart from my great happiness in getting married, I felt that it was time I did something more useful with my life.

After this my sister Mary arranged for me to stay with some great friends, Lord and Lady Barnard, near Catterick. Mary told them I had 'a great friend' at Catterick Camp whom I should like to ask for dinner and this was duly arranged — but on the evening in question Lord Barnard had to be at a Boy Scout function and Lady Barnard was away acting as hostess for her relative Lord Middleton. When Lord Barnard returned after dinner to find 'my friend' was none other than Prince Henry, he was mortified.

Over the next few days we had a lovely time motoring about the neighbourhood, visiting the local antique shops with an eye to our needs for a future home and eating in sleepy country inns. The engagement was not yet public but, although Prince Henry must have been recognised, nobody rang the Press or disturbed us in any way. In those days, of course, there was not thought to be any need for people in the public eye to have bodyguards or detectives for their protection, and even Mr Baldwin, the Prime Minister, used to spend his holidays on walking tours of Shropshire, often on his own, so that he was better able to gauge the opinions of ordinary people.

We had still to break the news to my father. He was so ill by then that we were worried about the effect it might have on him, but when I did finally broach the subject he seemed much calmer than I was and said he had guessed it for sometime. He did ask me if I was quite sure I was up to the task because he knew how much I had enjoyed my

independence. If I married Prince Henry, I should have to accept that I was a servant of the Country.

The King was greatly pleased with the engagement. On 25 August, 1935, he wrote to my father from Balmoral:

> My dear John,
> I must send you a line to say how delighted the Queen and I are that my son Henry is engaged to be married to your third daughter Alice. When I met you at Lords the other day I should have liked to have mentioned the subject, but there were too many people in the room. I trust you have given your consent. Our families have known each other for so many generations now, that it gives me great pleasure to think that they will be more closely connected still. I have not met your daughter yet, but hope to do so soon & I am sure I shall find her charming, she will certainly receive a warm welcome from my family. I suppose, if you approve, the official announcement ought to be made soon, but I wanted to see my son first, I hope this week. I am sorry to hear about your operation. I trust you are feeling better now & more comfortable & will soon be able to go to Bowhill & get out of the heat of London, which you must be finding very trying. There are a few grouse here, but not very many.
>
> > With kind messages to the Duchess
> > Believe me
> > yr sincere of friend [sic]
> > > G.R.I

My mother and I were soon invited to Balmoral, and I had to borrow some suitable clothes from Angela. On the very first morning I found myself sitting next to the King at breakfast. 'What are you doing today?' he asked. 'I'm going stalking,' I replied, thinking that as I had been asked to stay with my fiancé it would naturally be assumed that I would do whatever he was doing. I did not mean that I intended to shoot, just that I would go with him. I could see the remark was not a success. We exchanged no further conversation and off I went stalking with Prince Henry. I was a very good walker so it was no effort to follow him. When I told him about the effect my announcement had had on his father, he laughed. I could not, it seemed, have made a worse *faux pas*. Ladies at Balmoral at that time were not even allowed

to watch the grouse shooting, so the idea that I was intending to go out stalking was beyond the pale. It later transpired that the King had been so surprised that he had not dared say anything.

The Court was much more formal in those days. One was expected to change for tea and again for dinner, when one would wear gloves and jewellery. Today only the most splendid state occasions call for tiaras but at that time they were worn relatively often. Such house parties as there were were not to the taste of the Princes as the King and Queen invited very few guests, and those who did come consisted of old people such as Sister Agnes (a Miss Cayzer), who was a particular favourite of the King and had started a hospital for officers in the First World War. The Princes were also very much in awe of their father. He was very fond of them and they were devoted to him, but he used to bark now and

OPPOSITE: The official engagement photograph at Balmoral. The court was much more formal in those days.

ABOVE: Back at Bowhill.

then, and nothing they did ever seemed quite good enough. Not surprisingly they were always happiest when staying away at places such as Drumlanrig.

Back in London I spent a good deal of time at Buckingham Palace so that the King could get to know me better. He was very ill by then, but apparently I amused him. During dinner he was inclined to go to sleep, and as my stories used to make him laugh I was always placed next to him. He was kindly and rather absent-minded and did not make much effort at conversation.

Queen Mary, having been such a close friend of both my grandmothers, was especially pleased with the engagement. She was glad to have another 'daughter', the Princess Royal being so far away in Yorkshire and the Duchess of York (now the Queen Mother) so busy.

The wedding was planned for 6 November in

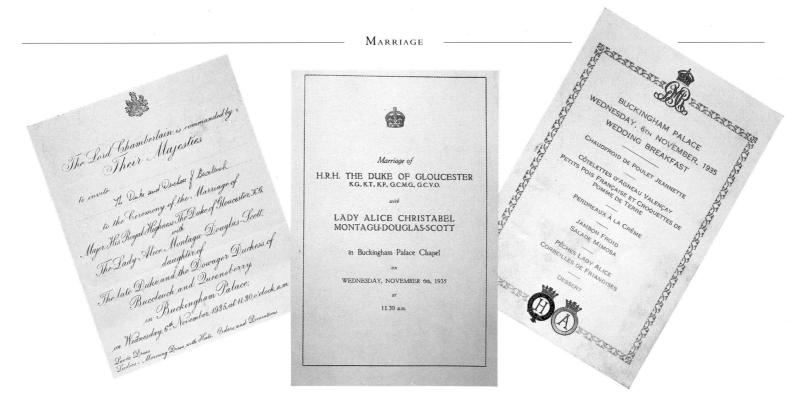

Westminster Abbey, but my father died on 19 October after a long struggle with cancer so all the arrangements had to be reconsidered. In the event, because the King himself was in such a fragile state of health, it was decided that we should proceed with the wedding but that the ceremony would be a private one in the chapel at Buckingham Palace.

It was a dark, drizzly day. A coach came to Grosvenor Place and Walter rode with me in place of my father. It was my first experience of large crowds and I found it a little frightening, but one knew one had to go through with it so that was that. After the wedding there was a breakfast, at which the King was visibly irritated by the difficulty we had in cutting through the rock-hard icing on the cake, and after that we came out on to the balcony. The Mall was thick with people as far as the eye could see, and thousands more cheered us all the way as we travelled in an open coach to St Pancras. The Duke of Kent's recent honeymoon had been considered too extravagant, so we were told to spend ours quietly in England. We could not think where to go but finally settled on Boughton, which was not lived in at that time of year. More crowds were out to greet us when we arrived, and the two miles

of road from Kettering to the Park gates was lined with people several deep on both sides all the way. There we did some hunting, much to Queen Mary's disapproval — she always considered it a highly undesirable sport — before travelling to Northern Ireland to stay with the Brookeboroughs for some woodcock shooting. Three days after the wedding I received the following letter from the King:

> Dearest Alice,
> Just one line to thank you for your charming letter & to say how touched I was by yr kind words, especially those about finding a new father to take the place of the one you have lost. I should love to try and take his place & I shall do everything to try & help you. Nice to think that you & Harry are having a little quiet & rest after the very strenuous days you have been living. But I fear yr weather has been very bad. Here it has rained every day since you left. We go down to Sandringham on Monday, by then I hope it will have improved & we shall be able to have a few days shooting.
> Wishing you every possible happiness
> Ever yr devoted father-in-law
> G.R.I.

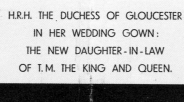

H.R.H. THE DUCHESS OF GLOUCESTER
IN HER WEDDING GOWN:
THE NEW DAUGHTER-IN-LAW
OF T.M. THE KING AND QUEEN.

The beautiful wedding gown worn by the LADY ALICE MONTAGU-DOUGLAS-SCOTT, now H.R.H. the DUCHESS OF GLOUCESTER, was a masterpiece of British design. It was carried out in deep ivory satin, with a wonderful pink pearl tinge, specially woven for the bride. Only the loose drapery of the corsage softened the unbroken lines of the gown, which had a knot of orange-

blossom at the neck. The wedding dress had a very long train, a wide sash, and a veil of cloudy tulle. The head-dress was a massed diadem of orange-blossom, each stem joined in silver thread. After the ceremony, the bouquet of roses and lilies-of-the-valley was sent to Westminster Abbey to be laid on the Tomb of the Unknown Warrior, as a tribute from the Duchess of Gloucester.

PHOTOGRAPHS BY FAYER OF VIENNA, DORLAND HOUSE.

RIGHT: A photograph of the wedding breakfast held at Buckingham Palace and, opposite right, the menu.

ABOVE: According to The Sketch *my Hartnell wedding dress was 'in deep ivory satin, with a wonderful pink pearl tinge.'*

I had eight bridesmaids.

I began to write letters to the 1,200 or so people and organisations who had been kind enough to give us presents. We had received so many lovely things: silver and jewellery from the King and Queen, the various wedding-cakes, a white ostrich feather fan from the Ostrich Farmers of South Africa and a Standard car, which we felt we had to return to the donor. There were of course more modest but no less touching presents from members of the general public. We were to receive a lot of presents in the years to come, many of them useless things like elephant tusks. The most lavish were probably those made by shipping companies when one launched a ship. They seemed to have a tradition of always giving jewellery.

Our honeymoon over we returned to Prince Henry's regiment at York, before spending a family Christmas at Sandringham. There was an incident at tea one day which I have always

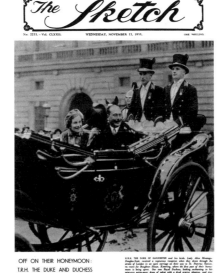

OFF ON THEIR HONEYMOON: T.R.H. THE DUKE AND DUCHESS OF GLOUCESTER.

To our surprise crowds also lined the road from Kettering station to Boughton.

remembered. Prince Henry always went everywhere with two little black Scotch terriers. They were not popular at Sandringham because the King's dog did not like other dogs, so they had to be kept out of sight. One day, however, they somehow appeared in the drawing-room at tea-time. Knowing how much this would upset the King if he noticed we hurriedly hid them under a table and told them to sit which they did until Princess Margaret came in. She was only three or four at the time and began to run round and round the table, whereupon one of the Scotties jumped out and bit her on the leg. Prince Henry managed to grab the dog before it was noticed and Princess Margaret, also knowing the dogs were not meant to be there, went very red but did not say a word, which was noble of her. She just disappeared to have her leg doctored in the nursery and soon returned none the worse.

The wedding group.

It was a rather sad Christmas with the King ill and the Prince of Wales away skiing in St Anton with Mrs Simpson. Prince Henry and I had also wanted to go skiing but were dissuaded because of the embarrassment if we had bumped into Mrs Simpson. However the chief anxiety was the King's ill health. Prince Henry was in bed with a very bad bout of influenza when the final summons came in the New Year, but I was able to arrive at Sandringham before the King died and to accompany Queen Mary back to London. On the drive from the station it was touching to see how many people took off their hats and bowed as a mark of respect as she passed. She was very upset but controlled as always. I had received a last letter from the King on 14 January.

My Dear Alice,

Many thanks for yr letter. What you say about the servants especially the butler is very funny. I am glad they are not yours. I hope you will find the pavilion at Aldershot warm enough. After very wet & stormy weather, we have got nice bright frosty days (11 degrees of frost) & they have been out shooting every day, unfortunately I don't yet feel fit enough to shoot & there is so much to shoot, last week in 5 days 5000 head. We have had various guests who come and go. The Gathorne-Hardy's are here now. Much to our regret George & Marina & their sweet baby left us this morning. Elizabeth is progressing, but very slowly & it may be some days before she can come here, as she is still so weak. Mary we expect next week for a few days.

With our love to you both

Always yr devoted Papa

G.R.I.

The paper is edged in black and the envelope sealed with black wax, in mourning for the King's sister, Victoria. It was written six days before he died.

The 'pavilion' was the Royal Pavilion at Aldershot, which was to be our home during Prince Henry's time at Staff College. It was a large wooden bungalow built for Queen Victoria to stay in whenever she came down for her military reviews. The house was raised about a foot above the ground on wooden piles and if you lay down, you could see across to the other side. Once one of our heavier guests plonked himself down in a chair and one of the legs went clean through the floor. Staff quarters and kitchen were down the hill and connected to the house by means of a lift and a passage. Food arrived in the dining-room none too hot.

It was a happy time. A comptroller looked after the finances, equerries organised our daily life and I had only to approve the menus. The change in my status did not alter my life very much. I found everyone bowing and curtsying rather embarrassing at first, but naturally I did not expect old friends in private to do such things or to call me 'Ma'am'.

Our official duties were negligible. I thought Prince Henry would tell me what to do, but if anything it was the other way round. He was a very vague sort of person, who hated fuss and bother, but was most particular in regard to the correctness of official dress or uniform. He liked nothing better than the army and outdoor pursuits and the greatest disappointment of his life was when the abdication forced him to abandon any hope of commanding his regiment, the 10th Hussars. But this lay ahead. When he had 'homework' I helped him colour the maps. We did not deceive the teachers. At the end of the course my handiwork was especially commended by the examiner!

Edward VIII, as the Prince of Wales had now become, often lived close by at Fort Belvedere with Mrs Simpson and they sometimes invited us over to dinner. This was awkward, as we were as unhappy with the liaison as the rest of the family, but as a brother Prince Henry felt obliged to go. Mrs Simpson was always charming and friendly and, being American, a wonderful hostess. After dinner we would play *vingt-et-un* or rummy or watch a film.

I happened to be dining with Queen Mary at Marlborough House when the matter finally came to a head. The King suddenly appeared

LEFT AND FAR LEFT: *A shooting lunch on the moors at Balmoral.*

LEFT: *The three sisters-in-law and my nieces off trout fishing in various modes of attire.*

after dinner. He was in a great state of agitation and asked the Queen if I could leave the room as he had a very serious family matter to discuss. Queen Mary was discernibly angered by this request but, with profuse apologies she asked me to go, which of course I did. Afterwards they came to fetch me, both very upset. 'I'm so sorry,' the Queen apologised again. 'It was so rude of us sending you away but David has told me some distressing news which you will know all about in due course.' It was not difficult to guess what it might be.

The abdication of Edward VIII promoted Prince Henry to the position of Regent Designate, which effectively put paid to his army career. Nevertheless we stayed on at Aldershot while York House, Edward VIII's home before he became King, was prepared for us. One of our visitors at this time was the Emperor Haile Selassie. He came with a son whom Prince Henry remembered from the imperial coronation some years before. 'How your little boy has grown,' he said to break the ice. This was interpreted and met with the answer, 'It's a habit little boys have.' After which conversation dried up. At another of these lunches the butler came round with the cheeseboard on which

there was a small cream cheese and offered it first, as protocol demanded, to the Emperor. Having no experience of such a thing, he took us all by surprise by removing the whole cheese, clearly under the impression that it was all for him. I had the embarrassing task of explaining to him that, as it was such rich food, only a small portion was usually taken by each guest.

In the autumn of 1938 I suffered a second miscarriage and the doctors ordered a holiday. We decided to go to Kenya. On the way back we stopped off for one night in Paris to see the Windsors. It was Neville Chamberlain's idea, not ours. The Government was still undecided about the Duke's future and, before reaching a conclusion, they wanted to test public opinion with news of our visit. The Windsors took us to dine in some smart restaurant, though I could not have felt less chic with the red dust of Kenya still in my hair. The event was given Press coverage and the response from the public made it clear to the Government that a reconciliation with the Windsors would not be popular. Meanwhile we received quite a lot of rude letters, an upsetting experience at the time.

Chapter Thirteen

BARNWELL

HAVING A 'GRACE AND FAVOUR' RESIdence in London at York House, we decided it was time to invest in a home of our own in the country. In 1938 we bought Barnwell Manor in Northamptonshire. Barnwell was a sixteenth-century building near the remains of a Saxon castle which today contains a tennis court. The property had been part of the Boughton estate until my father sold it for some reason in 1912 to a Polish family, who then sold it on to Captain and Mrs Cooper.

We liked the house immediately and its position near Boughton, in easy reach of several of the best English hunts and close by several friends with shooting estates, including my then brother-in-law David Burghley, could hardly have been better suited to our needs. We bought the buildings and four tenanted farms for £37,000, the greater part of the money left to Prince Henry by the King. When Prince Henry was appointed Governor-General of Australia in 1945, we sold the tenanted part of the estate for £47,000 and over the years since our return have succeeded in buying up land round about to the equivalent pre-war extent of 5,000 acres.

It was at Barnwell that we found ourselves at the outbreak of war in 1939. On 10 September I wrote to the Queen Mary:

OPPOSITE: *Prince Henry with William on the lawn at Barnwell. Above is a formal portrait of myself in WRAF uniform.*

It has been rather exhausting as the weather has been so close and 'muggy'. Harry and any available grooms, footmen, chauffeurs etc have been helping to load the wheat on to carts and to stack it. And Eva and various maids and myself have been putting the newly cut pieces into 'stooks'. We are covered with bites! From 'harvest bugs' I suppose ... I have been asked to have a Hospital Supply Depot here ... Each village has a working party and we shall have to send them the materials and patterns from here and then collect the finished articles to pack up and send off.

In the coming five years I was to visit hospital depots all over the country.

On 12 September Prince Henry was formally appointed Chief Liaison Officer, British Field Force, which took him to France on secret missions. He returned for a few days in November. The blackout was already in operation and one evening we delivered some top-secret papers to the War Office. While Prince Henry handed these over in person, I waited in the back of our official car. Suddenly Hore-Belisha, then Minister of War, came hurrying down the steps, mistook our car for his in the gloom and next minute found himself sitting on my lap. I was still giggling at the thought of it when Prince Henry came out.

This photograph was taken in 1942 at Badminton, where Queen Mary lived during the war.

It was extraordinary how quickly circumstances and attitudes changed. I wrote to Queen Mary that our horse-box had been appropriated as an ambulance and that 'numerous workmen still seem to wander in and out of the house finishing various jobs at their leisure. The War is made into an excuse for every thing.' It was also to extend my public duties considerably. By 1940 in addition to being Colonel-in-Chief of two regiments — The King's Own Scottish Borderers (KOSB) and the Northamptonshire Regiment — I was Commandant of the St John's Ambulance Brigade and Air Chief Commandant of the Women's Auxiliary Air Force (WAAF).

Queen Mary had been moved for safety's sake to Badminton, the home of the Duke of Beaufort, deep in the Gloucestershire countryside. Here she had a private suite of rooms, her own household and a platoon of soldiers as a bodyguard. She kept herself and the men busy by 'wooding' — a daily session of clearing a wood near the house of unsightly timber, fallen and standing. 'I hope you and Eva will help with the gardening in old clothes!' She wrote, before I visited her for the first time. 'We have got far beyond the ivy, whole trees and shrubs come down in no time.'

York House had been taken over by the Red Cross so when we had to be in London the King and Queen kindly put us up at Buckingham Palace. I was there the night Queen Wilhelmina of the Netherlands arrived from Holland. She had literally had to run from her palace in her dressing-gown and had somehow been spirited on to a British warship. Here she was, a forlorn figure, in little more than a mackintosh, with not a possession to her name — so much so that when the footman called in his customary way to ask whether I would prefer to dine alone or with the King and Queen, he added, 'Queen Wilhelmina may be joining Her Majesty, though only if a frock can be found for her to wear.' She was a rather large lady and none could be found big enough for her.

A great fear concerning the royal family throughout the war was that the Germans would kidnap us. However, in the event of this happening, never at any time were we given instructions what to do. The only protection against it as far as I was concerned was the arrival of a detective — a Welshman soon nicknamed the 'faithful corgi' — who came with his family to live at Barnwell, and accompanied me everywhere I went for the next five years.

At Barnwell the male servants and employees were conscripted into the forces, so I was left with only old people who, nevertheless, manfully dug up the greater part of the garden and turned it over to potatoes. It was sad to see the flower-beds that we had cherished destroyed in this way, but it was not a very serious sacrifice in the circumstances. My secretary kept rabbits which meant that we were forever picking dandelions. At the height of the Battle of Britain my splendid neighbour Lady Ethel Wickham gave a helping hand in shooting the partridges. 'It is wonderful that she can still tramp through the turnips at her age — I don't think she shot very many! But it was better than no other gun!!' Lady Ethel was ninety at the time.

In Victorian days Lady Ethel had been one of the best horsewomen and riders to hounds in England and rather frowned upon as a result. Her father, Lord Huntly, who was sixty when she was born, had fought at Waterloo and her grandfather danced with Marie Antoinette. She gave my eldest son William a redwood tree to plant because she thought it would be amusing for him in his old age to tell his grandchildren that it had been given to him by someone whose father had fought at Waterloo.

Lady Ethel was not the only local marksman. On 1 November I wrote to Queen Mary with news of my brother-in-law, Charles Phipps, 'who is over 50 and in charge of 16 anti-aircraft guns near Nottingham, which is really rather a good effort. He is a very slow and rather bad shot at pheasants, but we hope perhaps he may find German aeroplanes easier to hit!'

That autumn also saw the arrival of the first evacuee children at Barnwell. Two little boys came to stay in the staff quarters of the main house, now largely habitable after an almost total renovation, and their sister was lodged with the butler and his wife, who had a little house nearby. One morning the boys got up at 4 a.m. with the intention of walking the eighty miles back to London. They went in the wrong direction and were soon returned to the safety of Barnwell. Asked why they had run away, they said the country was dull and they wanted to see more of the raids and guns.

My worst experience of the bombing was having to tour Coventry two days after the dreadful blitz that destroyed so much of the town, including the old cathedral. As we visited one factory, an air-raid warning went off and the Lord Lieutenant, who was acting as my guide, asked me if I would prefer to go to an underground shelter or to continue the tour. I said I should much prefer to be bombed than buried, so long as it did not force other people to follow my lead. 'Splendid!' he said. 'It will set a very good example to the workers. They're apt to dash to the shelters at the slightest excuse.' So we continued the tour and luckily no raid materialised.

Prince Henry and I seldom undertook official duties together at this time, but a memorable exception was our visit to Belfast from 21–24 April, 1941. 'Lord Haw Haw' had said the Germans would never bomb Belfast, because they wanted to use the shipyards when they took over. Accordingly no one had bothered much with air-raid precautions, and the devastation was terrible. Our visit, as usual, had been planned in secret some time before; but as it coincided, quite by chance, with the day after the raid, we met with an extraordinarily grateful, even hysterical, welcome. The people were so overwhelming in their response that the police decided it was safer to let us walk among the crowds, which they would never have done in normal circumstances. Neither of us had ever witnessed anything like it; nor were we to again.

May brought confirmation that I was once more expecting a baby. On the 31st Queen Mary wrote: 'I was so thrilled and delighted at your good news this morning that I nearly fell off my dressing-table stool in my excitement!' She was very exercised on my behalf with everything to do with the baby and advised me on 22 July: 'Fortnum and Mason are so expensive that I think you had better go elsewhere for the cradle.'

A couple of weeks before the birth I wrote to her with more irritating news: 'A kind South African Doctor had sent me a case of oranges but Lord Woolton will not allow me to have it! Harry is furious! A rather curt letter came from Lord W's secretary to say that no one is allowed to send presents weighing more than 2 lb (about 5 oranges) so he regrets I cannot have them.'

William was born on 18 December. A delighted Prince Henry got compassionate leave for two days. On 9 February Queen Mary wrote to sympathise with me over his renewed absence. 'It is a pity Harry is so far away from you at present as I know what a lot of things you want to settle, things which one cannot do alone without one's husband's valuable advice, besides which it is so nice to talk things over together, don't you think so? That is what I miss so dreadfully for Papa and I always talked and discussed things.'

The Archbishop of Canterbury performed the christening at Windsor on 22 February. We chose the names William Henry Andrew Frederick. Prince Henry again managed to attend on compassionate grounds, before disappearing north again to his military duties. 'What a pity Harry will miss 3 months of the baby's adorable baby days which one simply loves,' commiserated Queen Mary, 'especially the first one. You cannot think how Papa enjoyed our first baby (that naughty boy!!!) he was always in and out of the nursery.'

Prince Henry was even farther away throughout the summer on a diplomatic mission to the Near and Far East and India. He returned unexpectedly, landing at one of the new American airforce bases near Barnwell, and as no one had been able decipher the coded notice of arrival, beyond the fact that it was someone of great importance, and because Cary Grant was rumoured to be on his way to the base as a rear-gunner, the Press gathered on the runway for a scoop. When they saw Prince Henry emerge they disappointedly said 'Oh, it's not him' and had vanished before he put a foot on the tarmac.

From Barnwell that autumn I complained 'that the weeds are terrible and our lawns all shaggy and unmown and the yew hedges covered with long whiskers!' Americans from the local aerodromes so enjoyed visiting the garden that soon we left it open for anyone to come and wander around. One fair-haired young airman particularly liked it and over the months earned some privileges like helping himself to fruit. He used to come regularly, so when one evening as I was hurrying back to the house to give William his bath I thought nothing of it when I heard his voice asking 'Can I look around again?' Not even when I turned to reply and could see no one there. Afterwards I learned that at approximately the time I 'heard' him he had been shot down and killed in a bombing-raid over Germany.

Meanwhile the baby prospered — rather too much for Queen Mary's liking. 'So William is walking already,' she wrote on 30 November, 'much too soon, don't let him get bandy-legged!' In the New Year I confirmed that 'he is always covered with bruises and scratches as he is very inquisitive and venturesome and will climb under and over and on to everything, usually in a hurry, and then trips over something and takes a crash! But he is very brave and never cries much — he loves animals and has no fear of them at all and gives carrots to the horses who put their heads right into the pram.'

In the autumn I took him to Scotland to see my mother at her new home of Branxholm, near Bowhill, where she had retired for her widowhood. Here, in old age, she continued to be as other-worldly as ever, telephoning Billy in a panic when her cheque-book ran out because she thought it meant she had no more money. With the years she had also become rather eccentric. When she opened her garden in the spring, she would pick great bunches of daffodils at Bowhill and then stick them in the ground back at Branxholm. As for the house itself, in due course she had a conservatory added, which served as both a sun-trap and dining-room but unfortunately had a very leaky roof. On one of our visits it seemed to rain incessantly and there we sat at every meal with one particularly persistent drip playing on the stoical Prince Henry's nose.

The airforce bases round Barnwell brought their own hazards. One day I was in my sitting-room when an aeroplane passed over very low, making a dreadful noise and trailing smoke and flames. William was asleep in his pram on the lawn. I rushed out and reached him just as the explosion from the crash shook the air. It must have been about a mile way, but the pram still leapt out of my hands. It remained upright and William appeared not to wake up; however, when Nanny Lightbody fetched him later he asked, 'Is aeroplane all right?' Another time when he was rolling about on a rug on the lawn a plane passed between the house and an old sycamore that stands about sixty yards away, knocking a branch off; amazingly the pilot managed to stay airborne and flew on.

The noise of the planes had a very noticeable effect on animals; and they could tell the difference between enemy planes and our own. At the beginning of the war all the hunters were commandeered for service in North Africa — a very sad moment — and we were left with two polo ponies, who both proved susceptible to the vibration of aircraft engines. If one of our planes passed overhead, they paid no attention but, when a German plane approached, they began to get fidgety and even to tremble. German engines made a different sound — anumb, anumb, anumb — and the ponies recognised this and associated it with danger. It was the same with the bull mastiff we had. He was terrified of German planes, wriggling under the bed or sofa as soon as he heard them coming. We were in the line of their raids to Coventry and the cities of the Midlands, and the shock waves from the bombs would set the pheasants crowing before we heard the distant 'crump' of the explosion. We were too far away for the house to shake,

but once an enemy plane jettisoned three bombs quite close by on its way back to Germany.

Like everyone else we tried to carry on as normal a life as possible. In the sporadic moments that Prince Henry and I were together we found our greatest relaxation in going out and helping on the farm. In 1943 Prince Henry was named to succeed Lord Gowrie as Governor-General of Australia and I discovered that I was expecting a baby. Richard was born on 26 August and duly christened Richard Alexander Walter George.

We left for Australia in December 1944 and for two and a quarter hectic years did not see Barnwell again. Almost the first official duty I performed on my return was to see the flood damage in the fens caused by the melting snows after the great freeze that winter. It was an extraordinary sight — mile after mile of water with just an occasional roof sticking out. At Barnwell everything was overgrown and sheep grazed the lawns, potatoes flourished in the rosebeds.

After a busy year, which included state visits to Malta and Ceylon, we had the joy of spending Christmas at home. The drawing-room, newly pannelled with Boughton oak to a design by Sir Albert Richardson, was much admired when, for the first time, we used it for the estate party. There too we 'saw in' the New Year; a year that was to be the first of twelve in which we rented Colin Mackenzie's House of Farr in Inverness-shire for the summer holidays.

We had a tutor for the boys, Mr Robson, whom we all loved dearly. He came each year, which was a great help as we knew he would keep a watchful eye if Prince Henry and I had to be away. There was always this wonderful feeling of blissful anticipation when

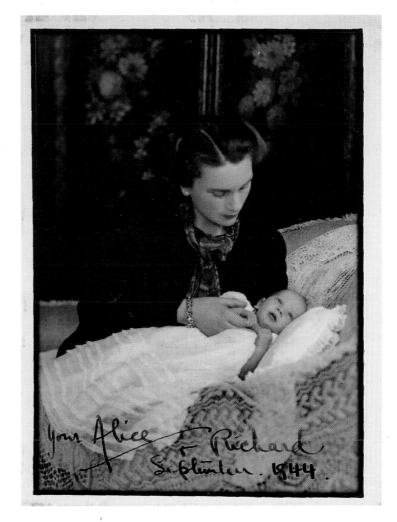

ABOVE: With Richard at Barnwell, 1944, and, above left, Barnwell in the spring.

On the lawn at Government House, Canberra, 1946. William shared my love of horses and riding.

the day arrived for us to set off on these northern pilgrimages. We usually broke our journey with a night at Drumlanrig or with my sister-in-law in Melrose. I think of these holidays as the happiest days of all, for which I shall forever be thankful.

The highlight was always the week we spent at Balmoral. Once, however, Richard was in a great state of agitation on our final day. It emerged that Princess Anne — then just five or six — had burst into his bedroom as he was packing, seized the dirk from his kilt stocking, and crying 'I've always wanted to do this!' plunged it into the eiderdown right through to the mattress. I told him he should have explained this to the Queen or the housekeeper, otherwise of course they would all think he had done it. But 'No,' he replied resolutely, 'I couldn't tell on her.'

Prince Charles and Princess Anne would visit us at Barnwell from time to time. When bicycling was still new to them, they loved to swoosh through the little ford in the village. With them came Nana Lightbody, who had been taken on by the Queen after leaving us.

Our boys were brought up with as little fuss and formality as possible. William was keen on riding, but Richard could not be

bothered to put on breeches and a cap and preferred his bicycle. I used to take them hunting occasionally which I think they enjoyed. Certainly it was less worrying for them than it was for me, with William going one way and Richard another. After the war we decided not to buy hunters again and kept one stableman only to look after our two polo ponies, our hacks and the children's ponies. Prince Henry and I would ride round the estate every morning whenever possible, and often the boys would come with us. Prince Henry also took great interest in teaching them to shoot. He was happy in joining them in outdoor occupations — croquet, bonfires, picnics, cricket — leaving me to do most of the indoor entertaining, like reading stories.

Cricket matches were always a tradition of the early days of August. There was an annual fixture with our neighbours, the Wolseley Lewis's, which usually ended up with both teams in the swimming-pool. There was also an annual Barnwell v. Sandringham match. The XIs consisted of all ages, old and young. With so many growing boys there were inevitably some surprises. One summer the Barnwell policeman's little boy missed the fixture because he had measles, but the following year he appeared as an unrecognisable six-foot tall young

In front of the old castle at Barnwell.

The children with my mother at
Branxholm, her home in the Borders.

Picnic at Norfolk Island, 1945.
The whole population attended —
all eight hundred descendants of
the nine mutineers from
The Bounty.

man and proceeded to bowl at frightening speed to the alarm of the Sandringham supporters. We were very embarrassed and signalled frantically for William to take him off, but he paid not the slightest attention. Luckily there were no casualties.

The children's preparatory and Eton schooldays were comparatively quiet ones for us. We both enjoyed country life and at Barnwell found plenty to occupy us in those moments when we were free of public duties. I always wrote my own speeches but Prince Henry seldom did and disliked delivering them just as much. He was the sort of person whom it was difficult to get started on time. He would never be ready but would be fussing over details, looking for papers and remembering last minute instructions. Even when we visited the boys at school we would sometimes arrive an hour late. I would be in agonies on the journey, thinking of them waiting forlornly, wondering what had become of us. No doubt they knew perfectly well.

Some events were a particular strain for Prince Henry and in consequence for me also perhaps the Trooping the Colour, for which he had to wear an uncomfortable uniform and ride a horse that probably hated the elaborate harness and trappings, was the worst.

Many functions, such as agricultural shows, we used to attend together. Prince Henry particularly enjoyed race meetings which held personal memories for him such as Aldershot races and the Grand Military Cup, which is now run at Sandown. After his death, I presented a trophy in his memory to be raced for at Sandown at the Grand Military meeting.

While Prince Henry concentrated on the farm, I kept an eye on the garden. He worked there too from time to time, especially when he could cut down some bushes, but only if I was with him as it bored him to do it on his own. We enjoyed buying antiques for the house and doing the rounds of the London shops in search of his favourite netsuke, miniature elephants, sporting prints, pictures and books. His favourite bookseller never much appreciated my coming as I would question the prices, whereas Prince Henry paid whatever was suggested without a murmur. 'Oh goodness,' I would say, 'we can't afford that, we really can't!' The bookseller would give me a withering look; but then next time he might say casually, 'Oh, by the way, I've found a rather less expensive copy of that book we were looking at on your last visit' — and produce no doubt the same one for our inspection.

The King's death in 1952 at such a relatively young age was a shock to us all and a great blow to Prince Henry, who was devoted to his brother and relied greatly on his good advice. The King was also an understanding and kind-hearted brother-in-law to me. It was typical of him, although he did not like writing, to send me a long and comforting letter the moment Prince Henry was despatched abroad at the beginning of the war.

A year later we were again filled with sadness by the death of Queen Mary. The Duke of Windsor stayed with us at York House for the funeral, and there was one evening when the Princess Royal came to dinner and the sister and two brothers sat up till the early hours discussing old friends and past times. It was particularly moving listening to the Duke because he was so obviously pleased to be talking with his own family again.

However, our spirits were soon raised again by the Coronation. We must have been up by 5 a.m., getting the boys dressed in their new kilts and coats and ourselves in robes and orders. Prince Henry rode in the procession, while we shared a carriage with the Princess Royal who told funny stories to the boys when their spirits began to flag. It was a memorable day but a long one.

The new reign found us as busy as ever. On an official visit to Africa in 1958 we met up with Haile Selassie again. We were delayed by fog, which puzzled him very much as he did not know what a fog was. Prince Henry inspected a Guard of Honour on our arrival at the palace. He sensed something large and hot sniffing at his heels and when he had a chance to look behind him, having reached the end of a row, discovered he was being followed by an apparently unattended lion. Luckily it was a pet of the Emperor and well fed.

After Ethiopia we went to what was then Somaliland. A memory of the visit was of an old chief telling us how sad he was at the prospect of independence, because he and others of his age could well remember how terrible the old days had been before British rule. I heard the same view repeated on other occasions during our many travels to the colonies over the years. But it was no use. The chiefs' sons would not listen. I suspect many of them would agree with their fathers now.

In England one of Prince Henry's favourite tasks was to give away the prizes at Wellington College. He always made a point of going by helicopter because it gave the boys the fun of seeing their parents' hats blown off. In the course of a year there would always be numerous official banquets. Winston Churchill enjoyed sitting next to me because he knew he would get double rations of champagne. I do not drink, but I would let my glass be filled so that Winston could have the benefit of it when he had finished his.

In 1962 we celebrated William's twenty-first birthday with a dance at Barnwell. The Queen brought her train to Barnwell station and very helpfully put up a number of people for the night. Unfortunately crowds gathered at a local level-crossing, causing an unprecedented traffic jam and delaying many of our guests. The dance also served as a climax to William's final year at Cambridge. He had enjoyed his time as an undergraduate, but came down feeling unsatisfied academically so chose to prolong his studies at Stanford University in California.

Richard in turn went up to Cambridge. 'Owd' you find Cambridge?' asked a pressman when he arrived. 'Look it up on a map,' he replied. He had no more idea of what to read than William had had, but took his older brother's good advice that it was best to do something one enjoyed. He had always been good at making models so William suggested he do architecture. This proved such a success that I am sure he would have become well known as an architect had he not had to succeed to the title.

When the time came for Richard to have a party it was a less formal affair. The house was placed out-of-bounds so as not to disturb Prince Henry who had suffered the first of several strokes by then; but there was an open-air film in the castle and three different bands. At about 11 p.m. I did a tour with my lady-in-waiting to see that everything was all right. There were some odd noises coming from the swimming-pool, so we investigated and found the only person there was a young rock musician, playing his guitar. 'Oh dear, has it gone wrong?' I asked. 'Nothing's gone 'wrong'', he said indignantly, 'it's meant to be like that.'

We also came across one young girl dressed like a pre-war debutante, in a beautiful ball-gown with long white gloves and pearls. Her mother had obviously assumed it would be a royal ball and had made her daughter dress accordingly. I felt very sorry for the poor girl as most people were dressed in a motley collection of their grandparents' clothes, a fashion of the time, and straw bales acted as tables and chairs.

Princess Anne came to stay for it. I think it was her first party away from home and I doubt if she has been to another like it. At about 4

OPPOSITE: *Off for a walk.*

This memorial plaque of William is in Barnwell church.

With William in Lagos. At the time William was Third Secretary to the Foreign and Commonwealth Office.

a.m. I woke up to the sound of cuckoos. It was as if every cuckoo in Northamptonshire had gathered to try and drown the noise of the band that was still pounding away in the distance. Looking out of my window I saw several Arabs floating around in white, playing croquet, which completed the strangeness of the moment. Some of the guests quartered themselves in tents and caravans in a field beyond the stables, and for a month afterwards I would find glasses and beer cans among the shrubs and plants as I went about my gardening.

As Prince Henry was now no longer able to carry out his public commitments, I had to substitute for him as best I could; and, as I never liked to leave him for long, this meant much tiring travel back and forth from Barnwell. William helpfully sacrificed his budding career in the Foreign Service to come home and take up Prince Henry's public and private responsibilities.

He arrived in 1970. He had been abroad so much — in America, Africa and Japan — and his leaves had been so short that I felt I had hardly known him as a man. The sad thing was that even after his return I still saw much less of him than I would have liked because in the evenings, when we might have taken a stroll together with the dogs

or I might have watched him play polo, I invariably had to be with Prince Henry so that the nurse could have the evening off.

Happily both William and Prince Henry shared in the happiness of Richard's wedding to Birgitte van Deurs. This took place at Barnwell rather than Birgitte's home in Denmark so that Prince Henry could be present, at least for the reception. A month or so before the great day Richard, Birgitte and I had joined William in Kenya for a brief and happy holiday. I stayed at Deloraine while they travelled around the country.

In a matter of weeks William fatally crashed his plane in an air race. He was always such a restless, active person that I have often wondered if he had some premonition that his life was destined to be short. Princess Alice happened to be staying with us for her annual visit. No one could have been of more comfort at such a time. Having lost her own son in a car crash, she knew only too well what I was feeling.

On the day it happened my oldest cousin, Sir David Scott, drove over from Boughton with a letter of sympathy, having heard the news on the television. His only son had been killed with the army in North Africa at the age of nineteen. Letters of condolence were overwhelm-

RIGHT: *Richard and Birgitte with my grandson Alexander.*

OPPOSITE: *Holding the Blesma rose — the rose of the British Limbless ex-Servicemen's Association.*

ing. I realised through them that sympathy is as great or even deeper than love or admiration.

Prince Henry survived William by two years. The great thing was to give him the comfort of knowing someone was there — if not the nurse, then myself or someone familiar to him, Mrs Holland my lady-in-waiting in those days or Lady Seton, then my secretary at Barnwell; or Prater and Amos, our chauffeur and butler for virtually the whole of our married life. Alice Saxby, the retired matron of King Edward VII's Hospital was another who sat with him and it was on her recommendation that we employed Sister Anne Greville as a nurse. Sister Anne became almost one of the family during her seven years of service with us, and with her sense of fun could make Prince Henry smile and laugh and look quite happy at times.

His greatest joy was to tour the farms in the Minimoke we bought. I also found some sort of peaceful happiness driving him on these occasions. When harvest time arrived and the great machines went back and forth, we would sit with the dogs and watch for ages. This sight seemed particularly to please and satisfy him and in some strange way I too found it very soothing.

Prince Henry no longer with me, William no longer around — no more holidays in Scotland, no horses to ride — I seemed bereft of so much that had brought happiness into my life. Thankfully I still had Richard, now married to Birgitte, and the welcome arrival of three grandchildren: Alexander, Davina and Rose. They have been the greatest joy to me. For a time I thought of retiring to Barnwell, but with the weeks and months that idea receded. I took up my royal duties again, sustained by the continued warmth and kindness of the many people I met with everywhere.

Throughout my public life I have often wondered why such crowds should come to welcome me, both in my own country and overseas. Was it to see what clothes I might be wearing? Or if I had a pretty face? Or was it that I represented something that lay deep-rooted in their hearts, a loyal and loving respect for any member of their royal family? This last I knew is the true answer. To anyone who reads this book and who has been one of those people in the crowds that have gathered to welcome me on such countless occasions, I would like to say thank you here for all the help and confidence you have given me to perform the public duty it has been my great privilege to fulfil.

THE MONTAGU DOUGLAS SCOTTS

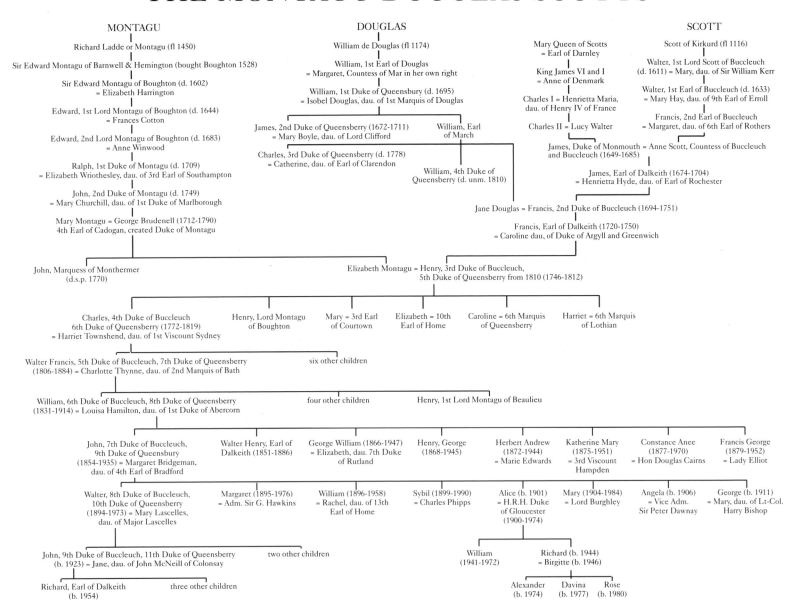

MONTAGU

Richard Ladde or Montagu (fl 1450)

Sir Edward Montagu of Barnwell & Hemington (bought Boughton 1528)

Sir Edward Montagu of Boughton (d. 1602)
= Elizabeth Harrington

Edward, 1st Lord Montagu of Boughton (d. 1644)
= Frances Cotton

Edward, 2nd Lord Montagu of Boughton (d. 1683)
= Anne Winwood

Ralph, 1st Duke of Montagu (d. 1709)
= Elizabeth Wriothesley, dau. of 3rd Earl of Southampton

John, 2nd Duke of Montagu (d. 1749)
= Mary Churchill, dau. of 1st Duke of Marlborough

Mary Montagu = George Brudenell (1712-1790)
4th Earl of Cadogan, created Duke of Montagu

DOUGLAS

William de Douglas (fl 1174)

William, 1st Earl of Douglas
= Margaret, Countess of Mar in her own right

William, 1st Duke of Queensbury (d. 1695)
= Isobel Douglas, dau. of 1st Marquis of Douglas

James, 2nd Duke of Queensberry (1672-1711)   William, Earl
= Mary Boyle, dau. of Lord Clifford   of March

Charles, 3rd Duke of Queensberry (d. 1778)
= Catherine, dau. of Earl of Clarendon

William, 4th Duke of
Queensberry (d. unm. 1810)

SCOTT

Mary Queen of Scots   Scott of Kirkurd (fl 1116)
= Earl of Darnley

King James VI and I   Walter, 1st Lord Scott of Buccleuch
= Anne of Denmark   (d. 1611) = Mary, dau. of Sir William Kerr

Charles I = Henrietta Maria,   Walter, 1st Earl of Buccleuch (d. 1633)
dau. of Henry IV of France   = Mary Hay, dau. of 9th Earl of Erroll

Charles II = Lucy Walter   Francis, 2nd Earl of Buccleuch
                              = Margaret, dau. of 6th Earl of Rothers

James, Duke of Monmouth = Anne Scott, Countess of Buccleuch
and Buccleuch (1649-1685)

James, Earl of Dalkeith (1674-1704)
= Henrietta Hyde, dau. of Earl of Rochester

Jane Douglas = Francis, 2nd Duke of Buccleuch (1694-1751)

Francis, Earl of Dalkeith (1720-1750)
= Caroline dau. of Duke of Argyll and Greenwich

John, Marquess of Monthermer   Elizabeth Montagu = Henry, 3rd Duke of Buccleuch,
(d.s.p. 1770)   5th Duke of Queensberry from 1810 (1746-1812)

Charles, 4th Duke of Buccleuch   Henry, Lord Montagu   Mary = 3rd Earl   Elizabeth = 10th   Caroline = 6th Marquis   Harriet = 6th Marquis
6th Duke of Queensberry (1772-1819)   of Boughton   of Courtown   Earl of Home   of Queensberry   of Lothian
= Harriet Townshend, dau. of 1st Viscount Sydney

Walter Francis, 5th Duke of Buccleuch, 7th Duke of Queensberry   six other children
(1806-1884) = Charlotte Thynne, dau. of 2nd Marquis of Bath

William, 6th Duke of Buccleuch, 8th Duke of Queensberry   four other children   Henry, 1st Lord Montagu of Beaulieu
(1831-1914) = Louisa Hamilton, dau. of 1st Duke of Abercorn

John, 7th Duke of Buccleuch,   Walter Henry, Earl of   George William (1866-1947)   Henry, George   Herbert Andrew   Katherine Mary   Constance Anee   Francis George
9th Duke of Queensbury   Dalkeith (1851-1886)   = Elizabeth, dau. 7th Duke   (1868-1945)   (1872-1944)   (1875-1951)   (1877-1970)   (1879-1952)
(1854-1935) = Margaret Bridgeman,   of Rutland   = Marie Edwards   = 3rd Viscount   = Hon Douglas Cairns   = Lady Elliot
dau. of 4th Earl of Bradford   Hampden

Walter, 8th Duke of Buccleuch,   Margaret (1895-1976)   William (1896-1958)   Sybil (1899-1990)   Alice (b. 1901)   Mary (1904-1984)   Angela (b. 1906)   George (b. 1911)
10th Duke of Queensberry   = Adm. Sir G. Hawkins = Rachel, dau. of 13th = Charles Phipps   = H.R.H. Duke   = Lord Burghley   = Vice Adm.   = Mary, dau. of Lt-Col.
(1894-1973) = Mary Lascelles,   Earl of Home   of Gloucester   Sir Peter Dawnay   Harry Bishop
dau. of Major Lascelles   (1900-1974)

John, 9th Duke of Buccleuch, 11th Duke of Queensberry   two other children   William   Richard (b. 1944)
(b. 1923) = Jane, dau. of John McNeill of Colonsay   (1941-1972)   = Birgitte (b. 1946)

Richard, Earl of Dalkeith   three other children   Alexander   Davina   Rose
(b. 1954)   (b. 1974)   (b. 1977)   (b. 1980)

INDEX

Illustration acknowledgements
8 © Weidenfeld and Nicholson Ltd.
157: © Times Newspapers Ltd.